DAVID WILLIAMSON's first full-length play, *The Coming of Stork*, premiered at the La Mama Theatre, Carlton, in 1970 and later became the film *Stork,* directed by Tim Burstall. *The Removalists* and *Don's Party* followed in 1971, then *Jugglers Three* (1972), *What If You Died Tomorrow?* (1973), *The Department* (1975), *A Handful of Friends* (1976), *The Club* (1977) and *Travelling North* (1979). In 1972 *The Removalists* won the Australian Writers' Guild AWGIE Award for best stage play and best script in any medium and in Britain, Williamson was nominated the most promising playwright by the London *Evening Standard*.

The 1980s saw his success continue with *Celluloid Heroes*, (1980), *The Perfectionist* (1982), *Sons of Cain* (1985), *Emerald City* (1987) and *Top Silk* (1989); whilst the 1990s produced *Siren* (1990), *Money and Friends* (1991), *Brilliant Lies* (1993), *Sanctuary* (1994), *Dead White Males* (1995), *Heretic* (1996), *Third World Blues* (1997, adapted from *Jugglers Three*), *After the Ball* (1997), *Corporate Vibes* and *Face to Face* (both 1999).

Williamson is widely recognised as Australia's most successful playwright. Over the last thirty years his plays have been performed throughout Australia and in Britain, the United States, Canada and many European countries. A number have been adapted for the screen, including *The Removalists*, *Don's Party*, *The Club*, *Travelling North*, *Emerald City*, *Sanctuary* and *Brilliant Lies*.

Williamson has won the Australian Film Institute film script award for *Petersen* (1974), *Don's Party* (1976), *Gallipoli* (1981) and *Travelling North* (1987), and eleven Australian Writers' Guild AWGIE Awards. He lives on Queensland's Sunshine Coast with his wife, writer Kristin Williamson.

ALSO BY DAVID WILLIAMSON FROM CURRENCY

After the Ball
Brilliant Lies
The Club
Corporate Vibes / Face to Face
Dead White Males
The Department
Don's Party
Emerald City
The Great Man / Sanctuary
Money and Friends
The Perfectionist
Siren
Sons of Cain
Third World Blues
Top Silk
Travelling North

COLLECTED PLAYS VOLUME I: *The Coming of Stork*; *The Removalists*; *Don's Party*; *Jugglers Three*; and *What If You Died Tomorrow?*

COLLECTED PLAYS VOLUME II: *A Handful of Friends*; *The Club*; *The Department*; and *Travelling North*.

ABOUT DAVID WILLIAMSON

Brian Kiernan, *David Williamson: A Writer's Career*
This authoritative account of Williamson's phenomenal career draws on his early writings, unpublished drafts, letters and journal entries; as well as the recollections of friends and colleagues.

THE REMOVALISTS

David Williamson

CURRENCY PRESS · SYDNEY

CURRENCY PLAYS

First published in 1972 by
Currency Press Pty Ltd
PO Box 2287, Strawberry Hills, NSW 2012
www.currency.com.au, enquiries@currency.com.au
Reprinted in 1973, 1974, 1975, 1977, 1978, 1979
New edition 1980
Reprinted in 1981, 1983, 1984, 1986, 1989 (twice), 1991 (twice), 1992, 1993
(twice), 1994, 1995, 1998, 2000 (twice), 2002, 2004, 2005, 2007

NATIONAL LIBRARY OF AUSTRALIA
Card number and ISBN   978 0 86819 038 9 (paperback edition)

Designed by Kevin Chan
Printed by Ligare, Riverwood

Contents

Don Crosby as Simmonds and Martin Harris as Kenny in the Nimrod Street Theatre production, 1971, directed by John Bell. Photo by Robert Walker.

Reflections on Violence

I sit down to write this brief introduction to David Williamson's powerful play, and in come two student friends. So I ask them whether they have any comment to make about violence in Australian society, and they reply: "I don't know, man. It's really peaceful."

The next day is Anzac Day. I spend the morning watching the march on the TV and wondering about its significance. Is it an elegiac demonstration for the dead? Or an affirmation that a man defines himself as a man only by his response to violence?

That afternoon, I am at the Melbourne Cricket Ground, yelling abuse at the umpire along with 40,000 other football fans. On the field, the players deal out and receive the usual quota of thumps behind the ear and short arm jolts. In the outer, there's a brawl during which a dozen young men are arrested. Am I externalising my violence, finding a socially-approved outlet for my aggressions?

And this morning a shudder of moral outrage reverberates through the Melbourne *Age*, as distinguished Australians indignantly reject Sir Phillip Baxter's suggestion that, in the event of nuclear war in the northern hemisphere, we might have to use force to prevent the nation being flooded and destroyed by nuclear refugees.

The Removalists raises three questions: one socio-cultural (is Australian society violent of its essence?); one political (do the forces of "law and order" rest on violence?); one psychological (do all of us have the kinds of aggressive instincts or behaviour patterns which Williamson depicts?).

Certainly Australian society was born in violence. The brutality of the convict system, the way in which it

corrupted prisoners and gaolers alike, are too well
known to require detailing here. Yet, only thirty
years after the baptism of New South Wales with
the gallows, the triangle and the lash, Commissioner
Bigge could report that the "sins" of the convict
fathers had not been visited on their sons.

The overt violence of convictism disappeared once
Australia became a colony of settlement, and little of
that inheritance — except perhaps an inbuilt dislike
of or distrust for authority — remains.

At the public level, Australia seems an extra-
ordinarily peaceful society. Of course there have been,
and are, exceptions. The Eureka Stockade. Occasional
clashes between troops or police and striking workers,
in which — on rare occasions — lives have been lost;
more recently, clashes between police and political
demonstrators. The gang warfare which surfaces
from time to time from the criminal underworld. The
street warfare, the bashings and pack rapes which
have emanated from the larrikin "pushes", the mods
and rockers, the sharpies, the bikies.

But compared with the savagery of the American
Civil War, of labour and race battles in the United
States, of gang and street warfare in the U.S. and the
United Kingdom, Australia does seem a strangely
non-violent society. To me, it lacks the "feel" of
violence.

True, I think of Sydney as "feeling" more violent
than Melbourne (which may be merely because I am
more aware of — and therefore avoid — those areas of
Melbourne in which violence is most likely to
surface). But compare any Australian city with, say,
Glasgow — a terrifying urban jungle in which the
rawness of the buildings and of workaday life is
matched by a twitching raw nerve of violence — and
Australia seems a society which is at peace with

itself.

One immediate reservation must be made. Australians
have successfully repressed memories of the most
violent episode in our history, the virtual annihilation
of the great majority of the 300,000 Aborigines who
occupied this continent before the Europeans arrived.
Unlike the frontier war waged by European settlers
against the American Indians, the Australian frontier
war was a piecemeal affair: the destruction, bit by
bit, of a people whose culture and technology made
it impossible for them to mount an effective (and
dramatic) resistance. Partly for that reason, and
partly because the Australian frontier did not exist
beyond the writ of law, and was never a place where
right and justice grew out of the barrel of an indivi-
dual gun, a Western-type film could never be made
about the Australian outback.

So one must conclude that Australia is – and thinks of
of itself as – a more peaceful society than most. And
if one asks why, one must answer that, at most times
in our history, Australians have thought of themselves
as a homogenous society, sharing a common culture
and common social aspirations. The class war has
been muted by economic well-being. The Australian
people have assumed a common objective: One
Continent, One People, One Culture.

But that is all at the public, surface level. It seems to
me that David Williamson (like Kenneth Cook in
Wake in Fright and Alexander Buzo in *Norm and
Ahmed*) has put his finger on a pulse of violence
existing at deeper levels in Australian society. Sometimes it surfaces in the sound of a bottle being
broken in a pub or in a random bashing outside a
suburban milkbar. More often it is latent, finding
expression in outlets which are socially approved
or in mores which are unthinkingly accepted socially.

At a Melbourne football ground, I watched a short-back-and-sides white-collar type take the beer can from his lips for long enough to address himself to the umpire: "You fucking poofter commo mongrel Jew bastard," and then get on with his drinking. That encapsulated most of the Australian prejudices (only "long-haired" and "unwashed" were missing). I believe that there are tremendous prejudices and pressures towards conformity in Australian society, reinforced by an implied threat of violence, from which we are saved only because most Australians are, happily, lazy. Football barracking is a socially approved outlet for aggression; the brawl which I witnessed (from a safe distance) at the M.C.G. is a-typical of Australian football crowd behaviour, in sharp contrast with the violence of roving packs of skinheads after soccer matches in the U.K.

At the level not so much of approval, but rather of unthinking social acceptance, I believe that the male-female relationship in Australia rests on a frightening sub-stratum of violence. Part of it is that the Australian culture belongs with Judaeo-Christian culture, which, as Joachim Kahl points out in *The Misery of Christianity*, is fundamentally anti-woman. The popular language of sex (as in all the variants of the English language) is violent. The deep repressions and frustrations expressed by Sergeant Dan Simmonds in his outburst against Kate and Fiona are endemic in this culture. There may even be other countries in the world where people go around systematically cutting out the female nipple from a poster advertising the magazine *Rolling Stone*. But beyond that the Australian code of aggressive masculinity (which found its first expression in "mateship") involves the positive isolation of women in their role as sexual objects. This implies an inhuman violence in sexual relationships, against which Women's Liberationists are quite reasonably protesting.

Again, there is perhaps in Simmonds' attitude to his junior, Constable Neville Ross, something of the aggressiveness expressed (for understandable reasons, more often vocally than physically) by the old towards the young. This reflects the deep and bitter resentment felt by the old against the challenge to their moral and institutional power. It is answered in turn by that cult of violence through which

some sections of the youth sub-culture express their socio-political frustrations, their positive desire for parental rejection. There is a point where youth violence and youth non-violence meet - the angry rejection of that violence meted out by an older generation through the superior technology they have created and controlled in Vietnam and elsewhere in the Third World.

by courtesy of the Daily Mirror

Once a pattern of violence is accepted for any circumstance, it becomes acceptable in all circumstances. Simmonds and Ross use Kenny as a punching bag in order to work out their own repressions and frustrations, and they can do so because they (or at least Simmonds) have come to take their own power as a matter of course. But that is not an evil peculiar to Australia; power is a cancer that eats at the heart of all civilised society. It can only be cured when a new society is created, one which would recognise the unique rights of all individuals, and generate ways of living in which the agressions which now pervade our community would simply not be needed any longer.

Ian Turner
1972

Authority and Punishment

The Australian Inheritance

1825 - 1840

"It was in the case of a government servant belonging
to a magistrate near me. The man . . . had got a drop
of liquor from a travelling dealer; his master's son a
very pert young fellow, began to curse and threaten
him; the man retorted; a constable was sent for,
whom he knocked down and escaped from. He then
ran off into the bush, taking with him . . . about three
parts of a cake he had by him ready baked. The young
fellow prosecuted him for drunkenness, insolence,
theft (the piece of bread, for rations are considered
the master's till used), and bushranging; and then the
magistrate made the constable swear the assault
against him. He got twenty-five lashes for drunkenness, twenty-five for insolence, fifty for bushranging,
six months to an iron-gang for stealing the cake, and
three months for assaulting a peace-officer in the
execution of his duty. The flogging he got before
going to the iron-gang frightened him; and on receiving sentence for some trivial offence at the iron-
gang, he escaped before the punishment was inflicted,
took to the bush, joined a gang of bushrangers who
had arms, committed several robberies with them, was
taken with arms in his hands, and hanged. The man
was a quiet, hardworking, honest fellow; but he could
not stand flogging."

*This tale was given by an immigrant gentleman
("through misfortune reduced to the inferior condition of a farm overseer") to Alexander Harris, who
retails the story in his book* Settlers and Convicts,
*the account of Harris' sixteen years in New South
Wales after his arrival in 1825.
With many other observers, Governor Macquarie
among them, Harris believed that the flogging and*

*other harsh treatment of convicts lead directly to
their "taking to the bush".*

1834
*John Jenkins, escaped convict and bushranger, mur-
dered former newspaper proprietor-editor Dr. Robert
Wardell on his Petersham estate; with his accomplice
Tattersdale and another condemned man he was
hanged at Darlinghurst on November 12, 1834. The
following day* The Sydney Herald *gave this account
of the execution:*

The extraordinary and reckless conduct of the culprit
Jenkins on his trial made, such an impression on the
minds of the Public, that, on Monday morning last,
the time appointed for his execution, the neighbour-
hood of the gaol was crowded to a degree never
before observed on any similar occasion, to witness
the last scene of one of the most depraved of the
human species . . . The prayers being ended, the Under
Sheriff read the warrant which consigned them to
their fate; when Jenkins ascended the ladder with the
greatest expedition, and on arriving on the scaffold
went over to one of the ropes suspended from the
fatal beam, and struck it with his hand in a playful
manner; the dreadful preliminaries being ad-
justed, Jenkins addressed the felons in the yard to
the following effect; "Well, goodbye my lads, I have
not time to say much to you; I acknowledge I shot
the Doctor, but it was not for gain, it was for the
sake of my *fellow prisoners* because he was a tyrant,
and I have one thing to recommend you as a friend,
if you take the bush, *shoot every tyrant* you come
across, and there are several now in the yard who
ought to be served so. I have done several robberies,
and for fear that any innocent man should suffer on
my account, I have made a confession to the gaoler
. . . I have not time to say any more lads, but I hope
you will all *pray for me*." This address being ended,

the rope was secured round his neck, and the other
culprits shook hands, but Jenkins turned away from
Tattersdale with disdain, and said something like "let
every villain shake hands with himself", at the
solicitation of the Rev. Mr. McEncroe, he consented
to shake hands with him, and as he approached his
unhappy companion in crime, who appeared to be
absorbed in prayer, and making the most pious
ejaculation, he said "come come, my lad, none of that
crying, it's no use crying now; we'll be all *right* in
ten minutes time," he then gave him a hearty shake
of the hand, and took his stand. The clergymen
having retired, and arrangements being complete,
the platform fell, and the world closed on one of the
most ruthless assassins that ever infested the Colony.
The case of these Convicts shew in a striking point
of view, the absolute necessity for an unrelaxing
system of restraint on the Convict population.

*During the Victorian gold rushes unrest developed
among the diggers because of the imposition of
heavy licence fees - one pound a month, and eight
pounds, later five, for twelve months - and because of
constant police harassment, with frequent arrests
for non-compliance. They had no political rights;
it was "taxation without representation."*

*In late November 1854 resentment surged up into
dramatic political action. Ten thousand diggers
massed and pledged themselves to campaign for
specific reforms; at a later meeting many burnt
their licences; and some hundreds, under the
elected leadership of Peter Lalor, massed and
drilled within the Eureka Stockade. In the early
hours of December 3 a mixed party of police and
military fired on them. Twenty-five diggers, three
privates and an officer were killed. The Governor,
Sir Charles Hotham, believed (wrongly) that the
trouble had been provoked by "professional*

NOTICE
TO
SPECIAL
CONSTABLES.

All those who have been sworn in as such are repuested to

Attend Immediately

at the POLICE OFFICE, Swanston-st., when they will receive Instructions and Badges of Office.

J. T. SMITH,

Swanston-street Police Office, Melbourne,
6th December, 1854.

Mayor of Melbourne.

BY AUTHORITY JOHN FERRES, GOVERNMENT PRINTER, MELBOURNE

by courtesy of the Mitchell Library

*agitators" and "foreigners", and (rightly) that
"the promoters of sedition" had "further things
in view than the repeal of the licence fee". In the
course of his official account of the matter he
recorded that:*

On the 14th Instant, the Mayor and Town Council of
Melbourne, presented me with an Address expressing
the assurance of their sympathy, for the position in
which I had been placed, and their resolution to main-
tain the supremacy of the Law . . . A Deputation from
Gentlemen representing the Squatting Interests of the
Colony, also waited upon me tendering their loyal
and undivided co-operation in the suppression of
sedition.

...Within another month, the Commission now
visiting the Gold Fields will have made their report
and by that I hope to be able to abide. But so long as
a Law, however obnoxious, and unpopular it may
be, remains in force, obedience must be rendered, or
Government is at an end.

It was not always Government, police or troopers who imposed unjustly repressive or brutal measures; sometimes it was the community itself. On the Lambing Flat goldfields in New South Wales in 1861 more than 2,000 miners, violently aggrieved at the influx of many toiling Chinese, marched with bands, flags and slogans to oust them from the diggings, proclaiming their rights "as freeborn Britons" to do so. Tents and stores were fired, goods plundered and many "unarmed, defenceless and unresisting"

by courtesy of the Mitchell Library

Chinese badly wounded; The Sydney Morning Herald
reported on July 20 that:

Some of the acts of barbarism said to have been
committed here were such, that Englishmen can
scarce be brought to credit that their countrymen
could be guilty of them - for who amongst the British
people could ever believe that men of their own
country - Britons, would take the Chinese pigtails
with scalp attached . . . Men, or rather monsters, on
horseback, armed with bludgeons and whips, with a
fiend-like fury, securing the unfortunate creatures by
taking hold of their tails and pulling their heads so that
they came with their backs to the horse and their heads
upon the saddle, and then cutting or rather sawing
them off, and leaving them to the fury of others who
surrounded them.

1880 - 1901
*During the great strikes of the early 1890s, when
the Labour movement suffered its early and crucial
defeats, the Queensland, New South Wales and
Victorian governments unequivocally supported the
employers, providing massive forces of police and
troops to harass the unionists, arrest and gaol them
and (in Melbourne, August 1890) to "fire low and
lay them out - lay the disturbers of law and order
out."*

*In Rockhampton, in May 1891, twelve striking
shearers were acquitted on the charges of picketing,
unlawful assembly and riot; then Judge Harding,
of the colony's Supreme Court, after detaining and
coercing the jury for three days, secured their
conviction for conspiracy, invoking an 1825 statute
which had been repealed in England. The twelve
were sentenced "leniently" to three years' prison
with hard labour.*

*Through the eighties and nineties the radicals and
nationalists fought for the cause of labour and fed
its spirit with brilliant stories, ballads and journalism.
But they fought greed and injustice on behalf of white
humanity only; in a famous paragraph (July 2, 1887)
the Sydney* Bulletin *exposed the paradox:*

By the term Australian we mean not those who have
been merely born in Australia. All white men who come
to these shores - with a clean record - and who
leave behind them the memory of the class-
distinctions and the religious differences of the old
world: all men who place the happiness, the prosperity,
the advancement of their adopted country before the
interest of Imperialism, are Australian . . . Those who
leave their fatherland because they cannot swallow the
worm-eaten lie of the divine right of kings to murder
peasants are Australians by instinct - Australian and
Republican are synonymous. No nigger, no Chinaman,
no lascar, no kanaka, no purveyor of cheap colored
labour, is an Australian.

*The beginning of the twentieth century and the
federation of the Commonwealth found inequity,
inhumanity and privilege still well entrenched in
Australian society. Offenders in the gaols still suffered
flogging and hanging; "law and order" still functioned
in the interests of privilege and wealth. The nationalists'
republicanism had failed; their racism succeeded. The
White Australia policy held sway, a particularly
chauvinistic, unjustly punitive form of authoritarianism;
and it was the work, not of government or vested
authority, but of the democrats themselves.*

Police: Authority and Privilege

Many complaints of assault have been made against the police, but few actual charges have been laid. Most of the assaults have taken place within the confines of police stations and have been witnessed only by police; not surprisingly, we have never yet heard of one policeman giving evidence against another in these circumstances. Victims are reluctant to complain or take legal action, because they fear reprisals of one sort or another.

If the person assaulted has a criminal record he feels that it is too easy for him to be framed, it isn't worth the risk. But even the respectable private citizen is usually disbelieved by the courts when it is a case of his word against the police. To succeed he must be able to produce strong independent evidence; and when the only witnesses were police officers that, of course, is impossible.

Other victims have not enough money to get legal advice, and even those who can afford it are likely to find that their lawyers are reluctant to initiate or advise criminal proceedings against police; they have a natural unwillingness to cross swords with established power. And there are also those who, because of failure and frustration in similar situations in the past, become overwhelmed by the hopelessness of it all. Understandably enough, they feel that since the brutality they have suffered comes from the police — that is, from social authority itself — they are blocked at every turn, and there is nothing they can do about it. The danger of course is that the impotent rage they feel will eventually be expressed in fresh acts of violence on other victims.

The result is that many brutal assaults by police have not only gone unpunished; they have not even been properly investigated. And this, regrettably, has often encouraged the sadistic policeman. He has known that he could probably bash with impunity, that his mates would stick by him, and that nobody would take the word of a man who was probably already convicted against the word of the police. Furthermore, he knew that if he did happen to leave marks on his victim, he could get in first — by laying a charge of assault, or of resisting arrest, to justify the bashing.

Two other factors help to give immunity to criminally violent police. Those law-abiding and decent members of the force — and they are the majority — have generally failed to take the action necessary to halt their law-breaking colleagues. At the same time the courts have not appreciated the vital issues involved and have been reluctant to cast doubt or suspicion on the police; any legal contrivance was felt to be better than having to admit, even to themselves, that there was any such thing as a lying policeman, let alone a criminal one. And the brutal policeman has been allowed to feel more confident; he can be certain that his word will be believed. In recent years many began to boast openly that they were above the law and could get away with anything.

But now, after several members of the force have actually been gaoled for assault on private citizens, the scene in Victoria is somewhat different: it seems that there is at least a partial breakthrough. Recently, in the notorious Collingburn case, a coroner's jury found that two policemen had a probable case of unlawful killing to answer. The two were later acquitted at their trial. At least the whole story surrounding Collingburn's death had been heard. In other recent cases, police have been charged with assault, found guilty and sentenced to terms of imprisonment; and this is not the full extent of the breakthrough. It does seem now that complaints and allegations of assault have lessened and that the conduct of the police has in many ways improved. But there is room for further improvement; the educational process from ignorance, through incredulity and scepticism to belief is, in our society, an extremely slow and painful one.

Unhappily, there are those in positions of power who have a vested interest in maintaining this ignorance. The reluctance of the Victorian Government to

by courtesy of the *Age*

initiate the abortion graft enquiry, even in the face of massive public criticism, is one obvious example. Governments must present images of integrity and wellbeing in the public service departments they control — their political power depends on it, and scandals provide fodder for the opposition parties. When such authorities refuse to acknowledge that the foundations of their society are not quite what they would hope and prefer them to be, they become partly responsible for corruption — and

by courtesy of the Age

violence — in sectors like the police force. Some of the men in authority have now been enlightened; others remain blind.

And if the law-enforcers do not themselves obey the law, and the authorities turn blind eyes to corruption, how can the citizen himself be expected to be law-abiding? He lives in an increasingly impersonal society, probably in an over-populated super-city which provides little scope for the expression, or even the development, of his individuality. He is frustrated, faced at every turn by a plethora of restrictions and controls; he has an overwhelming, though not necessarily conscious, desire to escape. He may excape through alcohol or drugs — or through violent behaviour. In his violence, he may be over-identifying with some steely, adventuring super-hero of the mass media. (If the citizen happens himself to be a police-man, he will feel these same frustrations, the same need for escape; the only difference is that he has a certain licence to use violence on behalf of the law.)

What is the answer? It is clear that law enforcement as we know it has failed. We cannot expect to imprison every person who commits a violent act; more realistic answers lie in the fields of education, and more humane, and human-centred, urban development. Given real choices and opportunities, people will in time develop for themselves a non-violent ethos. There is really nothing to suggest — as some of our beleaguered, frustrated politicians do constantly — that violence is an inevitable product of the "permissive society". The reverse may well hold; with more, and more genuine, personal freedom, there could be much less violence among us.

Frank Galbally
Kerry Milte
1972

THE REMOVALISTS

Above: Don Crosby as Simmonds. Below: Max Phipps as Ross, with Don Crosby, Jacki Weaver as Fiona and Carole Skinner as Kate in the Nimrod Street Theatre production, 1971. Photo by Robert Walker.

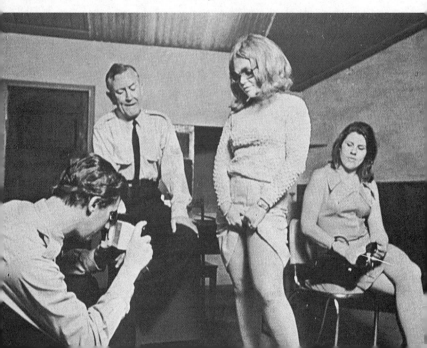

Ed Devereaux as Simmonds, Carole Mowlam as Fiona, Struan Rodger as Ross, Mark McManus as Kenny and Dalene Johnson as Kate in the Royal Court Theatre, London, directed by Jim Sharman. Photo by John Haynes.

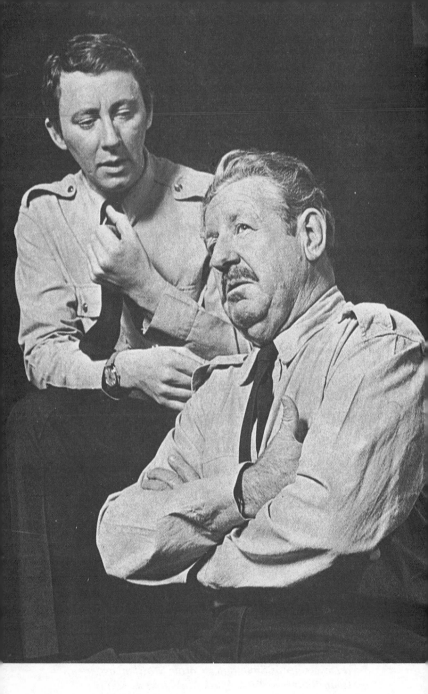

Gordon Glenwright as Simmonds and Max Phipps as Ross in the Playbox Theatre season, Sydney 1972, produced by Harry M. Miller and directed by John Bell.

*Above: Peter Cummins as Simmonds, Kate Fitzpatrick as
Kate and Jacki Weaver in the film* The Removalists,
*produced by Margaret Fink and directed by Tom Jeffrey.
Below: Ed Deveraux and Darlene John in the Royal
Court production. Photo by John Haynes.*

The Removalists was first presented at the Cafe La Mama, Melbourne, on July 22, 1971, with the following cast:

SERGEANT DAN SIMMONDS	Peter Cummins
CONSTABLE NEVILLE ROSS	Bruce Spence
KATE LE PAGE	Kristin Green
FIONA CARTER	Fay Byrne
KENNY CARTER	Paul Hampton
ROB, THE REMOVALIST	David Williamson

Directed by Bruce Spence

Martin Harris with Sandra MacGregor as Fiona in the Playbox Theatre production.

The Characters

SERGEANT DAN SIMMONDS

CONSTABLE NEVILLE ROSS

KATE MASON

FIONA CARTER

KENNY CARTER

ROB, THE REMOVALIST

*The play opens in a small inner suburban police
station built fairly recently but already having an air
of decrepid inefficiency. SERGEANT DAN
SIMMONDS, fat and fiftyish, lounges at a battered
old desk from which he surveys CONSTABLE
NEVILLE ROSS as if he were auditioning him for a
crucial role in some play. ROSS is twenty. There is a
long pause.*

ROSS: Well. What would you like me to do, Serg?

SIMMONDS: For a start you could stop bouncing up
　　and down on your bloody toes.
　　(Pause.)
　　D'you think they'll stop your paycheck if you're
　　caught standing still.

ROSS: *(nervously)* The pay's not too bad these days
　　is it?

SIMMONDS: *(looking at a crossword puzzle he has
　　been doing)* Magician in six letters, Ross.
　　(Pause.)
　　It's all right. I've got it.
　　(He writes something.)
　　The money is not good, Ross. The money could be
　　good if you happened to be in the right places but
　　this isn't one of them. No pay-offs here, boy. A
　　few perks but no pay-offs.

ROSS: A recruit under twenty-one gets full adult pay
　　these days. Did you know that?

SIMMONDS: How old are you Ross?

ROSS: Twenty.

SIMMONDS: Money's not important, boy.

ROSS: You've got to consider it.

SIMMONDS: You've got to consider your arsehole
　　too. What's your old man do for a crust?

ROSS: My old man?

SIMMONDS: Is he still alive?

ROSS: Yes.

SIMMONDS: What's he do?

ROSS: *(embarrassed)* Er . . . I'd rather not say.

SIMMONDS: *(irritated by ROSS'S reticence.)* God, he must be a nightman or something. Slinging shit.

ROSS: He's a carpenter.

SIMMONDS: What's wrong with that? Christ was a carpenter. Shouldn't be ashamed of your old man because he's a carpenter.

ROSS: I'm not ashamed of him.

SIMMONDS: No? I thought I noticed a little bit of hesitancy in your voice, boy. I thought it sounded as if you were ashamed of him.

ROSS: I'm not ashamed of him.

SIMMONDS: Is he in the building trade?

ROSS: No.

SIMMONDS: That's a pity. M'son's looking for a carpenter. He's sub-contracting his house. Are you going steady?

ROSS: Sort of.

SIMMONDS: Well when you get married make sure you don't go to a project builder.

ROSS: Why not?

SIMMONDS: Well just look at your project builder. What is he? Really?

ROSS: Dunno.

SIMMONDS: He's just a sub-contractor. Get me?

ROSS: I suppose he is.

SIMMONDS: Your project builder just hires your tradesman, and he isn't very particular about who he hires, either. No offence to your old man, Ross, but they've got carpenters working contract who couldn't drive a nail into a lump of fresh horseshit. M'son's worked it out that as well as being able to pick your tradesmen you can save yourself upwards of a grand.

ROSS: Sounds like a good move.

SIMMONDS: Like I say. It's better to save the stuff than to have to earn it. Pity your old man's not in the building game.

ROSS: Yeah.

SIMMONDS: Most of the carpenters I know are in the building game. Does he make furniture?

ROSS: *(thinking)* Er . . . no. Not exactly.

SIMMONDS: That's a pity. M'daughter's husband's looking for someone to knock up a few cupboards for him. They need 'em too. Five kids in seven years. Bastard's a mick. She's not but he's pretty strict. Ought to be kneed in the balls. So what if he's got to face the priest. She's the one who's got to have 'em. Can't stand micks. You a mick?

ROSS: No.

SIMMONDS: My wife's a mick. It's not her fault and I respect her point of view.
(Pause.)
They're taking over the force, you know. Salmon sandwiches on Friday if you want to get to be a sergeant, Ross. I told m'daughter not to marry the bastard but she couldn't afford to be choosy. Not

bad looking, mind you, and a good arse, but she's an irritable bitch. Her mother all over again.
(Pause.)
Pity your old man doesn't make furniture.

ROSS: Yes.

SIMMONDS: *(after a pause)* If he doesn't make houses and he doesn't make furniture, then what in the hell does he make?

ROSS: Why . . . er . . . did you want to know?

SIMMONDS: Is he the one that gave you this thing of yours about money?

ROSS: I haven't got a thing about money.

SIMMONDS: Then why were you carrying on about the pay?

ROSS: I wasn't carrying on about the pay. I just said that you've got to consider it.

SIMMONDS: *(looking at ROSS as he takes a roll of notes out of his pocket)* See that?

ROSS: Yes.

SIMMONDS: What is it?

ROSS: Money.

SIMMONDS: Where did it come from?

ROSS: I don't know.

SIMMONDS: I can walk out of this station tonight, grab m'self a cray and half a dozen tubes, get home, sit m'self down in front of the box and watch the wrestling.
(He waves the money.)
D'you know where it came from?

ROSS: No.

SIMMONDS: From my pay packet. That's where it came from. No pay-offs. No nothing. From my pay packet. D'you know why I'm never short of a dollar, Ross?

ROSS: No.

SIMMONDS: Because I've never been stupid enough to mortgage m'self up to the hilt. Bought m'self a little weatherboard in Box Hill nineteen years ago. Know what my repayments are?

ROSS: No.

SIMMONDS: Five dollars a week.

(ROSS whistles in admiration.)

SIMMONDS: Don't chase your arse boy. Get me? There's a lot more to be got out of life than chasing your arse. There's a good life here for you in the force if you know how to organise yourself.

ROSS: It's a pretty good life is it?

SIMMONDS: If you know how to organise yourself and get your priorities straight.
(Pause.)
Stuff the rule book up your arse. That's the first thing you've got to learn. Get me? Life's got its own rules.

ROSS: *(vaguely uncomfortable)* I ... er ... suppose this is a pretty busy station?

SIMMONDS: It could be if you let it be.

ROSS: How do you mean?

SIMMONDS: Just what I said. This district has got the highest incidence of crime in the metropolitan area.

(ROSS whistles.)

SIMMONDS: All your underworld is within a two mile

radius of this station.

(ROSS whistles again.)

SIMMONDS: Tough as nails around here, mate. I'd
    hate to think of the number of stiffs lying in shallow
    graves in the Dandenongs, courtesy of this district,
    boy.

ROSS: *(wide eyed)* Really?

SIMMONDS: *(nodding)* I reckon this'd be about your
    city's geographical centre of crime.

(ROSS purses his lips.)

SIMMONDS: That's why they opened up this sub-
    branch.
    (Pause.)
    To help the main station.
    (Pause.)
    And we do.
    (Pause.)
    But there's only two of us here. Right?

(ROSS nods.)

SIMMONDS: And we can't handle anything big. Get
    me?

(ROSS nods doubtfully.)

SIMMONDS: Get me?

(ROSS nods doubtfully.)

SIMMONDS: We can't handle anything big because
    there's only two of us.
    (Pause.)
    We can handle anything small, but then again its
    hardly worth the effort if it's small.
    (Pause.)
    The work load around here is very much a matter
    of how we see things, Ross. Something doesn't

have to be very big before its too big for us and
likewise something doesn't have to be all that small
before it's not worth worrying about. This is the
best posting in the city, boy. Think yourself lucky.

ROSS: What do we do then?

SIMMONDS: Anything that looks interesting. And if
there's nothing interesting *(pointing to a television
set)* we watch the midday movie. There's an old
Errol Flynn on today. Like Errol Flynn?

ROSS: How often do you get something that looks
interesting?

SIMMONDS: Depends what sort of mood you're in.
Some days just about anything's interesting. I
thought perhaps your arrival might have been
interesting.

ROSS: *(embarrassed by his lack of interest)* Oh I . . .
er . . .

SIMMONDS: Just joking, Ross.
(Pause.)
Got one boy posted out here who walked in and
said: "I've heard about you, you great fat heap of
shit". That was interesting.

ROSS: Why did he say that?

SIMMONDS: I hope you're not a young smart arse,
Ross, because there's no room for that here. There's
one person in authority here and that's me. Do you
understand, Ross?

ROSS: Yes.

SIMMONDS: Let's get that straight right at the outset.
(Pause.)
What's your father do?

ROSS: *(uncertain)* I don't think it's any of your

business.

(SIMMONDS gets up and circles ROSS.)

SIMMONDS: I thought we just had this out. Who's in authority here?

ROSS: I just don't think it's any of your business.

SIMMONDS: *(loudly)* Look Ross. I'm in authority here and I'll decide what's my business and what isn't my business.
(Pause.)
You're a bit of a rebel in your own quiet way. Aren't you? Makes you feel good?

ROSS: *(defensively)* No.

SIMMONDS: Doesn't make you feel good?

ROSS: No.

SIMMONDS: What? You just like being a rebel for the sake of being a rebel?

ROSS: No.

SIMMONDS: *(ominously)* I hope you're not going to turn out to be a smart arse, Ross. You'll go for a row of shitcans if you try anything smart with me, boy.

ROSS: *(surlily)* I just didn't think it was any of your business what my father does.

SIMMONDS: *(after a pause)* How long have you been in the force, boy?

ROSS: A year.

SIMMONDS: Not in training. In the force. In it.

ROSS: This is my first posting. You know that.

SIMMONDS: *(looking at his watch)* Half an hour. That's how long you've been in the force, boy. That's how long. Half an hour and you think you know what's my business and what's not.

ROSS: I don't think that at all.

SIMMONDS: *(after a pause)* Fail your Leaving?

ROSS: No.

SIMMONDS: We're starting to get a lot in who failed their Leaving. Got your Inter?

ROSS: *(embarrassed)* Got my Leaving.

SIMMONDS: *(raising eyebrows)* Is that a fact? Don't get many who've got their Leaving. *(Sarcastically)* You'll rocket to the top, boy. You'll be a sergeant by the time you're fifty-five. Why'd you join the force?

ROSS: Don't really know.
(Pause.)
I just thought I'd like to be a policeman.

SIMMONDS: So you joined the force? That's pretty smart, Ross. I can't think of many better ways of becoming a policeman than joining the force. I can see why you got your Leaving.
(Pause.)
You don't come from a broken home by any chance?

ROSS: No.

SIMMONDS: Last bloke who came here with his Leaving was from a broken home. Had a bit of trouble with him. *(Stating)* You're not from a broken home.

ROSS: No.

SIMMONDS: Yes. If your father's a carpenter he'd be pretty stable. People who work with their hands are always pretty stable. It's us bastards who work with our heads that go off.
(Pause.)

Yes. I tend to find that there are two types who
join the force, Ross. Bums and very smart men.
And when I'm talking about smart I'm talking about
the type of smart you've got if you can think on
your feet, not the type of smart that gets you good
marks in arithmetic. Get me?

ROSS: *(nodding)* I think so.

SIMMONDS: Bums and very smart men. I'm trying to
work out which category you fall into, Ross.
Why'd you join, boy?

ROSS: I just wanted to join.

SIMMONDS: All right. I'll just have to watch and find
out because it's an important thing to know. It's
important that I know as much about you as possible
because then I won't make mistakes. Will I? Eh?

ROSS: I suppose not.

SIMMONDS: We've got to work as a team, Ross.
There'll be times when we've got to operate like a
well oiled machine and that's the sort of thing they
can't prepare you for in training. What did they
teach you in training school? How to shoot a pistol.
Is that the sort of crap they taught you? Did you
learn that? Eh?

ROSS: Yeah. We did a bit of shooting.

SIMMONDS: And you shot at dummies. Eh? Ten
points for the heart, six for the liver. Bloody stupidity.

ROSS: You have to know how to shoot a pistol.

SIMMONDS: Next time you see a crim standing stock
still with a target painted on his heart you tell me,
Ross. They don't prepare you for the realities.
That's what I'm saying.

ROSS: We learned unarmed combat too.

SIMMONDS: What? They teach you how to shoot people then beat 'em up as well?

ROSS: You've got to be prepared for all eventualities. That's what I reckon.

SIMMONDS: That's what you reckon, eh?

ROSS: That's what I reckon. You've got to be trained for all eventualities in this rapidly changing world.

SIMMONDS: *(laughing)* Rapidly changing world. Did you swallow the brochures they gave you, Ross? Nothing changes in this world, boy.

ROSS: *(earnestly)* I think we have to be prepared for change in this day and age. I think our minds should be receptive to new ideas and new ways of doing things. I think that's most important.

SIMMONDS: *(slightly menacing)* Listen bonebrain. I have never drawn a gun in all my twenty-three years as a policeman. Never. If you ever let yourself get into a situation where you have to draw a gun, then you may as well get out of the force. What else did they teach you, Ross? How to make an arrest. Eh? How to make an arrest?

ROSS: *(sullen)* Yes. We learned that.

SIMMONDS: I have never made an arrest in all my twenty-three years in the force, Ross. If you ever get yourself into a situation that you can't handle without making an arrest, then you may as well get out too.

ROSS: *(aggressively)* What in the bloody hell do you do then? You never draw a gun, you never make an arrest. What in the bloody hell do you do?

SIMMONDS: *(menacing)* Don't yell at me boy.

ROSS: Well, what in the bloody hell do you do?

SIMMONDS: *(louder)* Don't yell at me boy.
  (Pause.)
  That's better.
  (Pause.)
  Now I want you to listen to me very carefully.
  Right?

(ROSS nods sullenly.)

SIMMONDS: Right?

ROSS: *(grudgingly)* Right.

SIMMONDS: You don't know a bloody thing. Right?
  (Pause.)
  You don't know a bloody thing. About life, about
  the force, about yourself. You don't even know why
  you joined up.
  (Pause.)

  I've been round on this earth about thirty years
  longer than you have, Ross, and in that time I've
  learned a lot of things. If you want to go on staggering through life like a blind man in a brothel, then
  that's your business. If your pride won't let you
  accept a little bit of hard-earned knowledge, then
  fair enough. You can go on staggering around for
  the rest of your life for all I care. Everybody's fool.
  Is that what you want?

ROSS: *(grudgingly)* No.

SIMMONDS: Good. We're getting somewhere. I'm glad
  you haven't got the sort of pride that won't accept
  a little bit of help. I'm glad you feel you can accept
  a little bit of advice.

ROSS: I'm always ready to accept advice.

SIMMONDS: Then how come you wouldn't tell me
  what your father does?

ROSS: I didn't think it was any of your business.

SIMMONDS: *(acting puzzled)* I don't understand you, Ross. You want my help. You want the benefit of my experience. You want to learn in a few years what it's taken me twenty-three and yet you won't - you will not - give me one simple straightforward bit of information about yourself. *(Acting angry)* How in the hell do you expect me to help you if I don't know anything about you?

ROSS: *(stubborn, sullen)* I didn't think you needed to know that.

SIMMONDS: *(emitting a long, weary sigh)* Yes. It probably seems irrelevant. Let me tell you a little story, Ross. A few years ago they sent me a young lad straight out of training - not unlike yourself. Wouldn't tell me anything. Fair enough. Either a person wants to tell me something or they don't. Two weeks after he arrived we got this hysterical little tart fronting into the station, yelling: "Rape". Quite common around here in the summer. At any rate we give her an aspirin, jump in the divvy wagon and cruise round a bit, and bugger me dead the lads in question were there, large as life, in the local hamburger joint. Well before I could stop him, the young fella's out the door and into 'em. Laid out three before I had time to park the car. Turned out the tart was the biggest bike in the district. They'd all been through her - no worries - but the only reason she'd stacked on an act was because the young idiots had left her out in the bush for a joke because they knew her husband was due home from night shift. Silly bitch panicked and thought she could square it with her old man by dobbing them in.

ROSS: What happened to the . . .

SIMMONDS: To the young fella?

(ROSS nods.)

Sued for assault. Out of the force like a shot. Wasn't anything I could do about it, Ross. Do you know why he snapped, Ross?

(ROSS shakes his head.)

His young sister was raped by a pack of bikies a few years before. At least that's what he was told, although personally I think there was something a bit fishy there too; but nevertheless the point is, Ross, that if he'd only confided in me it would never have happened. I would have been on the alert. Do you understand now why I have to know these things about you?

(ROSS nods.)

What does your father do?

ROSS: *(sullen)* He works for an undertaker. He makes coffins.

SIMMONDS: *(trying to suppress his laughter)* Coffin maker, eh? What's wrong with that? What's bloody wrong with that? I mean where would we be without coffin makers? Building a box to die in is every bit as important to the community as building a box to live in, in my estimation. Probably a bloody good craftsman to boot. People won't tolerate a shoddy coffin I can tell you that. Jerry-built houses - O.K.; but not a shoddy coffin. Why the hell were you ashamed of telling me that?

ROSS: I wasn't ashamed. I just didn't want to tell you.

SIMMONDS: Why? Because he deals with the dead?

ROSS: *(indignantly)* No.

SIMMONDS: *(insistent)* Because he deals with the dead?

ROSS: *(sharply)* No.

SIMMONDS: Everyone doesn't see the world the same
way as you do, Ross. That's one of the first things
you've got to learn. Everyone doesn't think there's
something odd about a man who makes coffins.
Hardly anyone thinks that. It's just a quirk of your
mind, boy.

ROSS: *(sullen)* I just didn't want to talk about him.

SIMMONDS: You've got your problems, haven't you?
Bit touchy about certain things, eh?

*(SIMMONDS stares thoughtfully at ROSS and doesn't
at first notice that two young women have entered the
station. The elder of the two, KATE MASON, is more
expensively dressed and more elegant than her younger
sister, FIONA CARTER; but FIONA has an easy and
innocent sensuality about her that is most attractive
and takes the edge from her sister's more conventional
beauty. KATE tends to be tense and affected. FIONA
is more relaxed and natural. The two policemen
notice them. SIMMONDS scrutinises them. There is
a pause.)*

SIMMONDS: Well. What can I do for you, ladies?

KATE: *(smiling)* My sister and I have come to report
an offence, Sergeant.

SIMMONDS: *(pulling a note-pad indolently towards
himself as he studies her)* Names?

KATE: I'm Kate Mason and this is my sister Fiona
Carter.

SIMMONDS: *(writing this down)* All right ladies.
(Grinning lecherously) Let's have it.

KATE: We've come to report an offence.

SIMMONDS: Against person or property, as they say?

KATE: Against my sister.

SIMMONDS: I see. What was the nature of this offence, Mrs *(checks pad)* Carter?

FIONA: *(calmly, matter of fact)* I was beaten by my husband.

SIMMONDS: *(putting down his pen and looking at ROSS)* Ross. This is Mrs Mason and this is Mrs Carter. Ladies, this is Constable Ross. He's just arrived from training school. I wonder if you'd mind if Constable Ross handled your case? Not because I think it's trivial, in fact just the reverse. I want Ross to get his teeth stuck into something substantial as early as possible. I tend to think it's a great mistake to throw a lad onto routine paper-work when he comes to you willing and eager.

KATE: *(smiling)* I would prefer to deal with the person in charge.

SIMMONDS: *(mock surprise)* Are you expressing a lack of confidence in Constable Ross, Mrs Mason?

KATE: *(forced smile)* Not at all, Sergeant . . .

SIMMONDS: Constable Ross is a product of the finest police training in the southern hemisphere, Mrs Mason. You've been thoroughly trained, haven't you, Ross?

ROSS: *(hesitantly)* I've been trained.

SIMMONDS: The boy's modest. Where did you come in your class, Ross?

ROSS: I did reasonably well.

SIMMONDS: Isn't he sweet? Where did you come, Ross?

ROSS: Ninth.

SIMMONDS: Out of how many?

ROSS: Eighty.

SIMMONDS: *(to KATE)* Top ten percent. *(Recalculating)* Almost. Pity you didn't come eighth, Ross. *(To KATE)* I think you'll find the Constable a very capable man.

KATE: *(forced smile)* I'm sure he is but . . .

SIMMONDS: I've judged Constable Ross competent to deal with your case, Mrs Mason, and in a way your objection to him is a reflection on my judgement.

KATE: It's just that . . .

SIMMONDS: Constable Ross has been prepared for every eventuality. Isn't that right, Ross?

(ROSS looks embarrassed.)

Isn't that right, Ross?

ROSS: Yes.

SIMMONDS: However I can understand your doubts and I feel that you're entitled to express them. After all, we are public servants. Servants of the public. I'll take charge. *(To ROSS)* I'm taking over, Ross. Two paces backwards and learn. Look and learn. *(To the women)* Right ladies, I'm all yours.

KATE: We appreciate your dealing with our case personally, Sergeant. My sister's rather upset over the whole business.

SIMMONDS: Yes. It's pretty terrifying when the family unit becomes a seat of violence.

KATE: *(fumbling in her handbag)* We've got a medical report from a doctor.

SIMMONDS: *(taking it and looking at it)* Your lawyer

told you to get this, I presume?

KATE: Yes, he did.

SIMMONDS: Then to come to us?

> *(FIONA and KATE nod.)*

I doubt if you'll get a conviction on the strength of this report, ladies.

KATE: It was quite a nasty bashing.

SIMMONDS: I'm sure it was but there's a saying in the trade: "Never arrest a wife basher if his missus is still warm". We don't like to stick our necks out on domestic issues for the simple reason that the wife invariably doesn't proceed. We could take him in for questioning.

KATE: Our lawyer said that even if you didn't arrest him you would make a report.

FIONA: Yes. We didn't so much want you to arrest him. We just wanted a report.

KATE: He said it was a pretty standard procedure.

SIMMONDS: *(not impressed with these references to the lawyer)* Yes, I bet he did.

KATE: *(still polite)* It will be all right won't . . .

SIMMONDS: Yes. Your lawyer's quite right.

KATE: Thank you, Sergeant.

(SIMMONDS takes a piece of paper, inserts it in the typewriter and shakes his head.)

SIMMONDS: Pretty standard procedure. Sometimes I wonder about lawyers.
(He bashes a few letters.)
I suppose their training makes them detached to a certain extent but I can't help wondering sometimes.

(He taps a few more letters.)
Your average lawyer's in love with procedures, I'm afraid. At this end of the law we're more interested in people. You'd be amazed at the range of our duties, Mrs. Mason. Your policeman isn't a numbskull flat-foot these days. He's a social worker, a marriage counsellor, a psychologist, a friend - you name it. There's an awful lot of cases that'd never go to court if the public trusted their police force a little more. Wouldn't you say, Ross, that the whole emphasis of a policeman's training these days is to enable him to handle human problems?

ROSS: Yes . . . well . . . we did do a subject called practical psychology for policemen.

SIMMONDS: Exactly. Did you find it helped your understanding of the human mind, Ross?

ROSS: *(shamefaced)* I was sick that week.

(SIMMONDS scowls at him and turns back to the ladies.)

SIMMONDS: The point about all this, ladies, is that I don't want to think I'm in the type of job where someone with a serious human problem can come in and all the help they'll get from me will be a few words typed out on a sheet of paper. I'd like to think that if there was something I could possibly do for them I'd do it. There's been a lot of broken marriages through this office, ladies, and the only good thing about that is that perhaps I've learned something that may be of assistance to someone else.

KATE: Well thank you very much, Sergeant, but I think perhaps that the report would be the most useful thing at the moment.

SIMMONDS: We don't always stick strictly to the letter of the law where human problems are involved, Mrs Mason. There may be some way we can help.

KATE: *(looking at FIONA)* Well we ... er ... do actually have one small problem ...

SIMMONDS: You tell me.

KATE: Well ... er ... Fiona has some rather gorgeous furniture that she went back to work to help pay for.

FIONA: That's not why I went back to work. I was bored stiff.

KATE: Nevertheless you did substantially pay for the furniture yourself ...

SIMMONDS: Look, I'm sorry ladies. Perhaps if we could start from the beginning. Where did you first meet your husband, Mrs Carter?

FIONA: *(looking at KATE who motions her almost imperceptibly to proceed)* In Germany.

SIMMONDS: Is he a foreigner?

FIONA: No. He's Australian.

SIMMONDS: I see. I take it you went overseas?

KATE: On impulse, Sergeant. She didn't even check to see whether she could get a job. When the whim took her she went.

FIONA: *(calmly)* That is not true, Kate. I'd planned to go for years and there were plenty of jobs around in England.

KATE: *(to SIMMONDS)* She ran out of money.

FIONA: It was stolen.

KATE: Well, you didn't cable me for more.

FIONA: Yes, well, I know what Ralph thinks of me.

KATE: Yes, well, Ralph knows what you think of him. Nevertheless he would have sent it.

SIMMONDS: Ralph's your husband?

KATE: *(nodding and smiling)* Despite what my sister says, Sergeant, the fact is that she did not think the whole thing out. She's always been a bit impulsive, I'm afraid.

SIMMONDS: *(who has moved close to FIONA and is ogling her)* Well, that can be a delightful fault at times, Mrs Mason. Are you a little bit impulsive too?

KATE: *(noticing THE SERGEANT'S attention towards FIONA, and starting to compete)* I'm afraid I am, a little bit.

SIMMONDS: *(savouring the possibilities)* Hmm. *(to FIONA)* And you met your husband in Germany, Mrs Carter?

FIONA: *(nodding)* In Munich.

KATE: At the beer drinking festival.

SIMMONDS: Yes. I've heard of it.

KATE: Hundred of Australians drinking themselves into a stupor. I don't know why they bother to go abroad. It's exactly the same as what they do back here.

SIMMONDS: *(to FIONA)* You met your husband at the festival?

FIONA: Yes. That's where my money was stolen. He was very kind to me.

KATE: Kind to you? He took full advantage of the situation.

SIMMONDS: *(ogling FIONA)* He . . . er . . . helped

you?

FIONA: *(matter of fact)* Yes. We lived together in London and got married just before we came home. *(Pause.)*
I was pregnant.
(FIONA smiles)
My pills were in the same handbag as my money.

KATE: *(irritated at being ignored)* It would've never occurred to her to abstain for a few days, Sergeant. *(She smiles at him knowingly.)*

FIONA: *(smiling)* Kenny told me he was clever.

SIMMONDS: *(ogling KATE)* What does your husband do for a living, Mrs. Carter?

KATE: *(determined to keep the SERGEANT'S attention)* That's a good question, Sergeant. Over there he was an overseas correspondent for the Herald. Back here it turns out that he's a mechanic who does the maintenance on their presses. Not that I object to his occupation. Just the lies.

FIONA: *(smiling)* I had a fair idea he was lying. He could hardly spell his name.

SIMMONDS: *(his eyes still on KATE)* And now he beats you?

KATE: You should see her bruises.

(SIMMONDS looks at ROSS.)

SIMMONDS: Actually that may not be a bad idea.

FIONA: *(dubious)* Is that necessary? We've got the medical report.

SIMMONDS: It could still help. If we can include in the report that the bruises were obvious even to the medically untrained eye it could lend a lot of weight.

KATE: *(gaining perverse sensual pleasure from the idea)* Show the Sergeant your bruises, Fiona.

FIONA: *(still dubious)* The largest one's on my back.

SIMMONDS: Let's have a look, then.

(FIONA hesitantly rolls up her sweater. SIMMONDS inspects her hips and back very slowly, prodding her flesh slowly and lasciviously. While he is doing this he occasionally looks across at KATE, establishing something of a carnal conspiracy between them. KATE is gaining sensual pleasure from THE SERGEANT'S lechery.)

SIMMONDS: Tender?

FIONA: *(flinching)* Yes.

SIMMONDS: *(prodding)* There?

FIONA: Yes. There.

(She flinches.)

SIMMONDS: Yes. I can see the discoloration. One of these braless birds eh?

KATE: Nature didn't intend us to wear bras, Sergeant.

SIMMONDS: Indeed nature did not. *(Putting an arm around FIONA)* I'll tell you this much, Mrs Carter. If I had a wife like you I wouldn't be beating her. *(Inspecting her closely)* Buggered if I'd be beating her.

KATE: *(looking at SIMMONDS)* She's got another bruise on her thigh.

(SIMMONDS bends down and hoists FIONA'S skirt up a little.)

SIMMONDS: Bit hard to see that one. Ah, there it is. Ross. Get out your notebook. *(To KATE)* We'd be

on much firmer ground if we got a bit of a sketch
or something. No. Look. I'll tell you what. Get out
the polaroid, Ross. *(To FIONA)* I wonder if I could
get you to roll up your sweater and skirt for a second
while Ross gets a snap of the bruises.

*(FIONA looks doubtfully across at KATE who gives
her an almost imperceptible all clear. It is a betrayal.
KATE wants the situation to continue for her own
amusement.)*

ROSS: Where do you keep the camera?

SIMMONDS: Do you know how to use it?

ROSS: *(smug and eager)* They taught us in training.

*(ROSS finds the camera and begins to take photographs.
SIMMONDS moves across and sits next to KATE who
is now sitting on the table. He puts his arm around her.)*

SIMMONDS: Domestic strife is an unpleasant business
for everyone concerned. *(To ROSS)* Do you think
you can handle it, Ross?

*(ROSS catches the air of sensuality and tries a heavy
handed pun.)*

ROSS: Handle what?

(He laughs raucously at his joke.)

SIMMONDS: *(tersely)* Take a close up of the one on
the thigh. *(To KATE)* I take it then that your sister
is going to use this evidence as grounds for divorce?

KATE: She will if she's got any sense at all.

FIONA: I just want a separation at the moment.

*(ROSS finishes taking the photographs and goes off to
see how they've turned out.)*

SIMMONDS: You're storing this evidence up for the
future then, Mrs Carter.

KATE: Or for the present if he tries to make trouble.

SIMMONDS: I see. *(To FIONA)* He's threatened reprisals if you leave, has he?

KATE: I'm sure he will.

FIONA: *(adjusting herself, speaking flatly)* I don't think he will.

SIMMONDS: Doesn't he know that you're leaving yet, Mrs Carter?

FIONA: No, he doesn't. I just decided.

KATE: We don't want him getting access to Sophie.

FIONA: *(To KATE)* I don't mind him getting limited access.

SIMMONDS: Sophie's your daughter, Mrs Carter?

KATE: Yes. She's a gorgeous child, Sergeant. Kenny scarcely knows she exists. We've found a charming little two bedroom flat in South Yarra for Fiona and the back room is just perfect for Sophie.

SIMMONDS: Sounds very nice.

KATE: Yes it's beautiful. The only reason we got it is that Ralph's a personal friend of Charles Weller the estate agent.

SIMMONDS: They're a very big firm, Wellers.

KATE: Ralph does his teeth.

SIMMONDS: Your husband's a dentist?

KATE: That's right

SIMMONDS: Well I wasn't far out. I had you tabbed as a surgeon's wife. Same money. More prestige.

KATE: I wouldn't say that.

SIMMONDS: No I'm afraid people think more of

someone who whips out their gallstones than someone who does likewise with their teeth.

KATE: Yes, well, we were very lucky to get the flat. The only bother is the ... er ... matter we were mentioning before.

SIMMONDS: The furniture?

KATE: That's right. It's gorgeous, Sergeant, but we're afraid that Kenny will try and hang onto it.

SIMMONDS: Do you think he will, Mrs Carter?

FIONA: I think so.

KATE: If he's forced to share it up he'll most likely sell the lot for a quarter of its replacement value, split the money and drink himself stupid for a week. We'd offer him a reasonable price for his half but we know he'd refuse. He's that sort.

SIMMONDS: *(To FIONA)* Come here, Mrs Carter. Sit down.
(He motions her to sit down on his free side. She does so with a little hesitation. THE SERGEANT now has an arm around both of the sisters. He assumes a fatherly air.)
Does your husband like the furniture, Mrs Carter?

KATE: Like it? Tell the Sergeant about the nights he came home drunk and said it made him want to vomit.

FIONA: *(with a half smile)* He usually did too.

SIMMONDS: Ross.

(ROSS approaches.)

ROSS: I think we'd better do these photographs again, Serge. The bruises didn't show up too well.

SIMMONDS: *(sharply)* Just put a circle round 'em

Ross. What I want you to tell me is what you'd think of a man who disliked certain items of furniture to the point of regurgitation and yet would sell them up rather than accept a generous cash payment for them.

ROSS: *(puzzled)* I don't know.

SIMMONDS: Well, unlike yourself Ross, I haven't had the benefit of practical psychology for policemen part one, but my native wit tempts me to attribute it to spite. Do you think it could be spite?

ROSS: *(shrugging)* I suppose so.

SIMMONDS: *(to KATE)* Ross is just feeling his way. Is there any particular night of the week when you can be reasonably sure that your husband won't be home, Mrs Carter?

FIONA: *(with some surprise)* Tonight. Friday's his drinking night.

SIMMONDS: Hmm. I think that we could get that furniture for you, Mrs Carter.

FIONA: *(looking dubiously at KATE)* Oh?

SIMMONDS: Suppose that Constable Ross and I organised a removalist to turn up at your flat tonight, helped you load the furniture, took you across to your new flat, helped you set it up, then went back and . . . er . . . pointed out to your husband that he's in no position to create any trouble because he's in great danger of being arrested for assaulting you.

KATE: *(looking at FIONA)* That would be marvellous. We wouldn't be putting you to too much trouble Sergeant?

SIMMONDS: No trouble at all.

FIONA: *(dubious)* Kenny's pretty bad tempered.

SIMMONDS: I think Constable Ross and I can handle that aspect. I'll drop in on you both from time to time after the shift to make sure Kenny isn't making a nuisance of himself if you like.

KATE: *(looking meaningfully at SIMMONDS)* I'd appreciate that, Sergeant.

SIMMONDS: *(looking at KATE)* Fine. Could we have your present address then, Mrs Carter?

FIONA: Flat three, fourteen Haughton Street, North Fitzroy.

SIMMONDS: Ah. Just round the corner. What time does your husband usually arrive home tonight Mrs Carter?

FIONA: Never before eleven.

KATE: And never sober.

SIMMONDS: *(to KATE)* I take it you'll be there to help your sister, Mrs Mason?

KATE: *(looking meaningfully at SIMMONDS)* Yes. I'd like to help her.

SIMMONDS: Good. I'll have the removalist get there early, say six thirty or seven, and that'll give us time to have a little bit of a flat-warming celebration before Constable Ross and I go back to speak to Kenny.

KATE: That would be fine.

SIMMONDS: Well, Ross. How does that sound? Are you free to give the ladies a hand tonight?

ROSS: *(embarrassed)* Well er . . .

SIMMONDS: *(sharply)* Well are you?

ROSS: Well I'd . . . er . . . like to help but I'd . . . er . . . arranged to er . . .

SIMMONDS: To what?

ROSS: I've . . . er . . . got something on.

KATE: *(not meaning it)* Oh we don't want to interfere with the contable's arrangements, Sergeant.

ROSS: *(blurting it out)* I wouldn't mind normally but it's me girlfriend's firm's night out. We're on the same table as the general manager.

SIMMONDS: *(wearily)* Ross.

ROSS: *(quickly)* I wouldn't mind normally but Marilyn me girlfriend's getting her hair set and I've paid a deposit on the tickets.

SIMMONDS: *(wearily)* Ross. One of the first things you've got to learn . . .

KATE: *(falsely)* We don't want to mess up the constable's arrangements.

SIMMONDS: *(to KATE)* He's got to learn that the force is not a nine to five job, Mrs Mason.

(He turns to ROSS and tries to make him aware of the sexual possibilities in the arrangement.)

Some of our most interesting work is done after hours, Ross. I'm afraid you're going to have to disappoint your young friend.

ROSS: *(thinking)* Will we get paid overtime?

SIMMONDS: *(wearily)* Yes, Ross. We will.

ROSS: *(more cheerful)* Might be all right then. She won't be as shitty if she knows I'm getting paid. *(To the women)* We're saving for the deposit on a house.

KATE: *(false smile)* How nice.

SIMMONDS: Well, ladies. That's it then until tonight.

KATE: We appreciate this very much, Sergeant.

SIMMONDS: *(shepherding them to the door, an arm around each)* Glad to be of help.

KATE: Until tonight then.

SIMMONDS: Until tonight.

FIONA: *(fairly flatly)* Thank you, Sergeant.

SIMMONDS: Glad to be of help.

(The women go. SIMMONDS looks at ROSS)

SIMMONDS: You stupid bloody nong, Ross.

ROSS: *(confused)* What've I done?

SIMMONDS: You stupid great arse. You nearly ballsed that. We'll be in like Flynn there tomorrow night. We'll thread the eye of the old golden doughnut - no worries.

ROSS: *(agape)* Do you think . . .

SIMMONDS: Do I think? All I can say, Ross, is that you better start conserving your energy right now. I'm having the dentist's wife. Snooty bitch but she goes for it. No worries.

ROSS: *(gravely)* Gee. I hope Marilyn doesn't find out.

(If an intermission is required it can be taken here. If not slides of the family life of ROSS and FIONA can be shown. ROSS with his proud family in his uniform. ROSS with Marilyn at last year's company ball. FIONA with KENNY and the babies. KATE holding FIONA'S baby, etc. The scene is now KENNY'S and FIONA'S flat. The time is six thirty that evening. FIONA is ironing in preparation for the shift. A large stack of cardboard boxes, in which she will pack small articles, are nearby. There is a bash on the door and KENNY comes in singing boisterously, carrying half a dozen beer bottles under his arm. FIONA looks up in alarm. KENNY goes to her and gives her a long gropy kiss which he evidently enjoys more than she does.

FIONA: *(edgy)* What are you doing home?

KENNY: Well, that's a lovely welcome. I do live here don't I?

FIONA: You don't usually come home on Friday nights.

KENNY: Unpredictable. That's part of my charm.

(He looks at her.)

　　What's wrong with you?

FIONA: Nothing.

KENNY: Well how about a bit of a smile then?

(FIONA tries a weak smile.)

KENNY: Christ. If that's the best you can do I'm going to watch the box.

(He takes his bottles across to the couch, puts them down, flops down himself, reaches for the automatic television operator and switches it on. He watches the programme for a couple of seconds, then turns round to FIONA.)

Chuck us the bottle opener.
(FIONA goes to a drawer in the kitchen.)
And a glass.

(She takes a bottle opener out of the drawer and reaches for a glass. She hesitates.)

FIONA: Er . . . I . . . er . . . wasn't expecting you home, so I haven't cooked any tea. Why don't you go and have a counter tea with the boys?

KENNY: Just knock us up a quick steak or somethin'. *(irritated)* Where's that bloody opener?

(FIONA takes him the glass and the opener.)

FIONA: Why don't you go and have a counter tea with the boys?

KENNY: *(looking at her with irritation)* I said knock us up a steak.

FIONA: I can't. I'm ironing.

(KENNY has another drink and watches the television for a second. He gets up and moves across to FIONA who irons nervously.)

KENNY: My God. You are ironing. Something must be wrong.
(He picks up something she has ironed.)
My God. *(looking at the ironing she has done)*
Don't notice anything of mine here, but I shouldn't complain. It's amazin' to even see you with an iron in your hand. Last time you ironed one of my shirts was two days before we were married.

FIONA: Why don't you go off and have a counter tea with the boys?

KENNY: *(angry)* What is this? Are you tryin' to get rid of me? A bloke decides to do the right thing and come home to his missus and he's no sooner in the door than you're tryin' to get rid of him. *(Suddenly suspicious)* Are you on with some other bloke? Is that why you want to get rid of me?

FIONA: Of course not.

KENNY: *(moves across and rummages through a pile of washing nearby)* Hey! Whose underpants are these?

FIONA: They're yours.

KENNY: *(belligerent, suspicious)* They are not mine.

FIONA: Don't be so stupid.

KENNY: *(taking the underpants across to FIONA)* They're not even my size.

FIONA: *(looking)* Yes they are. They're thirty-fours.

KENNY: Is that my size?

(FIONA nods and goes back to her ironing. KENNY still looks suspicious. He unbuttons his pants and pulls the tag on his present underpants into view.)

KENNY: *(triumphantly)* These are thirty-sixes!

FIONA: *(wearily)* They're the pair your mother brought you.

KENNY: *(deflated)* Aw.
(KENNY buckles up his pants and goes back to the television. He watches it for a few seconds then turns around.)
Knock us up a bit of steak, love.

FIONA: *(edgy)* Go and have a counter tea.

KENNY: *(getting up and moving to her, roaring)* Get out into the kitchen, open the fridge, get out a piece of sliced cow and put it under the griller, you lazy bitch.

FIONA: *(adamantly)* Go and have a counter tea.

KENNY: *(snaky)* No. You haven't got any man comin' in. It's just that you're too bloody lazy. That's what it is. Bloody slut.
(He sees the stack of cardboard boxes.)
What's these?

FIONA: *(nervously)* Boxes.

KENNY: *(roaring)* I can see that, you dumb twit.
(He kicks them, scattering them over the room.)
What are they bloody well here for? As if we haven't got enough mess already. What're they here for?

FIONA: *(nervously)* The . . . er . . . supermarket was getting rid of them. I thought they might come in handly.

KENNY: Handy for what?

FIONA: *(thinking)* For Sophie to play with.

KENNY: You're joking.

FIONA: She'll build houses and things with them.

KENNY: She'll rip 'em to bits like she ripped me bloody car manual.

FIONA: That was over a year ago.

KENNY: *(aggrieved)* They're out of print now. E.H. manuals. Can't get your hands on one for love nor money. Where is the little bugger?

FIONA: *(nervously)* She's over at my mother's.

KENNY: *(indignantly)* That old bitch has always got her.

FIONA: She hasn't had her for a fortnight.

KENNY: I was going to have a bit of a play.

FIONA: I'm sorry.

KENNY: I always have a wrestle with her when I get home.

FIONA: *(blowing up)* You're never home on a Friday.

KENNY: That old bitch does nothing but pump the poor kid full of social graces.

FIONA: Don't be stupid.

KENNY: Last time she was over there, when she came home she was running around saying: "Thank you. Please", like a little parrot, until I straightened her out.

FIONA: *(gritting her teeth)* For Christ's sake will you go down the pub with your mates!

KENNY: *(getting up from the television and moving to her with an air of conciliation)* Anyrate let's not argue. I didn't come home to argue.
(He feels her bum. It is obvious what he has come home for. She doesn't react.)
How about coming and watching some television?
(He feels her breasts and bum. She doesn't react.)
Come on. Might develop into somethin?

FIONA: *(edgy)* I'm not in the mood.

KENNY: *(still feeling her)* You were last night.

FIONA: *(flaring)* Yes, and then you bash me up straight afterwards.

KENNY: It wasn't straight afterwards, and it was about something completely different, and I didn't hit you that hard.

FIONA: Well, it hardly inspires confidence when you're made love to one minute and bashed up the next.

KENNY: *(taking his hands off her)* Look. I'd been warning you about that kitchen tidy for two days.

FIONA: Why didn't you empty it out yourself?

KENNY: *(indignantly)* That's your job. I can't understand how a mother could let the kitchen tidy get
in that state when she's got a young daughter whose
health might be endangered.

FIONA: What rot.

KENNY: Rot's the word. Apart from anything else
the bloody thing stunk.

*(Their noisy argument is interrupted by a knock at the
door or doorbell ringing. FIONA is anxious. She thinks
it is the removalist. KENNY stomps across to the door
and throws it open. KATE comes in. She is surprised
to see KENNY there and looks anxiously across at
FIONA.)*

    Migod. It's the ugly sister. To what do we owe this
unexpected pleasure?

KATE: *(ignoring him)* Hello, Fiona. Just dropped by
to see how you were.

KENNY: She's fine. Now piss off.

FIONA: *(to KATE)* Good to see you. Would you like
a cup of tea?

KENNY: Yes, and a bit of steak as well.

KATE: *(trying to be pleasant to KENNY. She sees he's
been watching the television)* What's that you're
watching?

KENNY: Television. It's a new electronic wonder
that's just filtered down to the lower classes. Keeps
their brains nice and soggy.

KATE: *(still even)* I thought you went out on Fridays.

KENNY: I heard you were coming so I stayed home.
*(Kenny gets up, storms past FIONA into the kitchen,
grabs a tin of baked beans and a can opener and a*

packet of sliced bread. He opens the can and stuffs beans and bread into his mouth, deliberately trying to disgust KATE. He washes the food down with generous draughts of beer from the bottle. He glares at KATE.)
Don't you like my manners?

KATE: *(coolly)* You'll get indigestion if you bolt your food like that.

FIONA: *(to KATE, giving frantic eye signals)* I told him he ought to have a counter tea down at the pub.

KATE: It would certainly be more nutritious than that junk.

KENNY: I've had about as much of this as I can stand. I think I will go down the bloody pub.
(He gets up and puts on his jacket. There is a rather imperious knock at the door, or a repeated bell ring. KENNY mutters and goes to answer it. A self assured REMOVALIST in a dust coat enters. The dustcoat is emblazoned with the emblem 'Aussie Removalists'. The two sisters look at each other in alarm. FIONA retreats toward the kitchen, followed by KATE. They busy themselves making cups of tea.)
What do you want?

REMOVALIST: What'd you think?

KENNY: How the bloody hell would I know?

REMOVALIST: Well read me bloody dustcoat.

KENNY: *(reading)* Removalist. I don't want no bloody removalist.

REMOVALIST: *(he has heard this story before)* Look boss. I just get me orders. I ring in and get me orders and this is where the girl sent me. I checked the address.

KENNY: Well check it again.

REMOVALIST: I checked it again.

KENNY: Well check it again because I don't want no bloody removalist.

REMOVALIST: *(getting irritated)* Look. Don't take it out on me, boy. I just ring in and get me orders. This is where I been sent and this is where I came. If you've changed your mind then be man enough to admit it and pay me me five dollars cancellation fee.

KENNY: *(scornfully)* Five dollars?

REMOVALIST: Give us five dollars and we'll call it quits.

KENNY: Don't be funny, mate. I don't want no removalist. Piss off.

REMOVALIST: I'm gonna do one of two things. I'm gonna take me five dollars and leave or I'm gonna start shiftin' furniture.

KENNY:*(getting angry)* Look. How many times do I have to tell you, mate. I didn't call no removalist.

REMOVALIST: We've had trouble like this before, mate. If you've changed yer mind and you don't want a removalist then give us your five dollars and I'll go. I've got ten thousand dollars worth of machinery tickin' over out there in the drive and if it ain't bein' utilized then that's money I've lost. Get me?

KENNY: *(losing patience)* Look mate. You've made a mistake. Go and check it out. I'm countin' to three and if you're not -

REMOVALIST: *(heated)* I know what's happened. It's happened to us before. One of them wog bastards has underquoted us, haven't they? They're cuttin' their own bloody throats, those wogs. Some of 'em work twenty hours a day seven days a week and if

they're shiftin' you, you better make sure you're
insured to the hilt, because they 'aven't any respect
for your property, mate. None at all. I've seen 'em
reduce an antique dresser to kindling more that once.
All haste and no speed.

KENNY: *(Ominously)* Finished?

REMOVALIST: Just warnin' you, mate.

KENNY: Well I ain't been underquoted by no one for
the simple reason that I ain't had no quotes for the
simple reason that I don't want nothin' shifted.

REMOVALIST: Well I'm sorry mate but we just don't
make mistakes like this. Everything is double checked
at both ends, and I ain't leavin' without me five
dollars and I've got the Transport Board regulations
to back me up.

KENNY; *(fed up)* Look. Piss off or I'll spray the back
of your throat with teeth.

REMOVALIST: Are you threatening me?

KENNY: No. I'm doin' a line for you, you thick bastard.

REMOVALIST: Go on. Take a swing, mate.   See what
happens. Take a swing.

*(KENNY snorts in disgust, slams the door, walks back
to the centre of the room.)*

KENNY: *(to FIONA)* Did you hear that nut?

FIONA: *(lying)* No. What did he want?

KENNY: You heard him, didn't you?

FIONA: *(nervously)* No, I was . . . er . . . talking to
Kate.

KENNY: *(still amazed)* Bloody removalist. Wanted to
shift our furniture out. Bet I know what's happened
too. Little tart who gives 'em the jobs is gettin'

back at him for doing the dirty on her. Or his mates have played a joke on him and he's too thick to catch on.

(The knocking at the door, or the bell ringing, starts again with renewed vigour.)

KENNY: *(pointing at the door, genuinely surprised)* There's the mad bastard back again. *(Calling out)* Piss off you idiot. *(To the women who look at each other , embarrassed)* I'm gonna hammer the bastard this time, I'm afraid.

KATE: Look, I'll go and . . . er . . . talk to him.

KENNY: *(motions her back)* No. Stay there. He's an idiot. No tellin' what he might do. You stay there.

(There is a crash as the door is burst open by SIMMONDS, whose momentum carries him on past a rather surprised KENNY. ROSS follows close at SIMMONDS' heel and practically comes face to face with KENNY, and despite his keenness shows some embarassment. THE REMOVALIST follows ROSS looking very nonchalant.)

KENNY: Hey. What's all this about?

SIMMONDS: All right Ross. Handcuff the bastard.

(Ross is obviously nervous and excited at what is his first taste of action. He clips the handcuffs on the bewildered KENNY, but in his excitement clips the other cuff to his own wrist.)

SIMMONDS: *(loudly)* Don't cuff him to yourself Ross.

(ROSS fumbles with his free hand to find the key, but without success.)

KENNY: *(bewildered, angry)* Hey. What's all this

about?

SIMMONDS: It's about beating your wife, Carter.

KENNY: *(looking at FIONA with surprise)* Beating my wife? All I done was give her a bit of a shove. You can't arrest a man for that. Never even hurt her.

ROSS: *(to SIMMONDS)* I think the key's in me back pocket.

(He sticks out his bum in SIMMONDS' direction. SIMMONDS considers this manoeuvre as being below his dignity and turns to KATE.)

SIMMONDS: I wonder if you'd mind getting the key out of Constable Ross's back pocket, Mrs Mason.

(KATE does so, looking at FIONA. They are both a little nonplussed. ROSS takes the key, undoes his handcuff, and handcuffs KENNY, who is still protesting, to a chair.)

KENNY: Christ, I only gave her a shove. She tripped and fell against the cabinet herself. You can't arrest a man for something she done herself. How would you like a kitchen full of stinking rubbish?

SIMMONDS: *(loudly)* Don't cuff him to a chair, Ross.

ROSS: *(defensively)* He can't get far with a chair.

SIMMONDS: *(tersely)* He can pick the bloody thing up and clobber you with it, bonebrain. Whack it on that table leg.

KENNY: Listen fellas. A joke's a joke. I won't shove her again.
(ROSS pulls KENNY down in order to cuff him to the leg of a coffee table. KENNY stands there awkwardly with a bent back. Eventually he sits down.)
Listen; fair go, fellas. What's the charge?

SIMMONDS: Resisting arrest, and two separate charges of assault.

KENNY: *(indignant)* Resisting arrest?

SIMMONDS: You assaulted this gentleman here *(indicating THE REMOVALIST)* then repeatedly refused to answer the door.

KENNY: *(incredulous)* Assaulted him? You ought to get your facts straight. He's some kind of nut. If you're looking for someone to arrest, then go him. Tried to con me out of five dollars. Mad as a bloody snake. I thought it was him at the door again.

SIMMONDS: I said: "Police here", twice, and you chose to ignore it.

KENNY: I only heard the banging.

SIMMONDS: *(to KATE)* Did you hear it?

KATE: *(flustered)* We were in the kitchen, Sergeant.

KENNY: *(to FIONA)* You bitch! Go and dob me in because I gave you a bit of a shove. *(To KATE)* I bet you've got somethin' to do with it, ferret features. What are you stickin' your nose in for?

SIMMONDS: *(kicking KENNY in the thigh)* That's enough of that kind of language, fella. *(To ROSS)* Book him for resisting arrest and using indecent language.

KENNY: What? Ferret features? That's not indecent.

SIMMONDS: Book him, Ross.

KENNY: *(outraged)* Cut it out. You can't walk into a man's house and kick him.

SIMMONDS: Book him, Ross.

ROSS: *(concentrating fiercely)* I am placing you under arrest on charges of resisting arrest, two separate

instances of assault, and using abusive, insulting and
obscene language. I must warn you that anything you
say may be taken into account and used against you.
I would advise you therefore to follow me quietly
to the station where you will be given the opportunity
to seek legal advice.

KENNY: *(to ROSS)* All right. Take me to the station,
you young Burke. Take me. I'll have your balls. The
two of you. I'll get Galbally and sue the arse off you.

ROSS: *(highly excited)* Don't talk to me like that, fella.
I'm warning you. I'm an officer of the law. Don't
talk to me like that. You come quietly, fella, I'm
warning you.

*(He unlocks KENNY and is about to cart him off.
KENNY is protesting volubly with such phrases as
'Jesus', 'This is supposed to be a free country isn't it,'
'Why don't you spend your time catching real criminals
for a change and get the bloody crime rate down.' The
dialogue is rather confused at this point, with lines over-
lapping and people talking at cross purposes.)*

SIMMONDS: Ross, you idiot. We haven't finished here
yet.

KENNY: *(to KATE)* You've worked this all up haven't
you, you bloody tight-arsed, would-be socialite.

SIMMONDS: *(loudly)* Don't cart him off yet, Ross.
Cuff him to the door handle.

KENNY: *(still talking to KATE)* You – – What in the
hell entitles you to go round stickin' your nose into
other people's affairs? And get that look off your
face.

*(ROSS and SIMMONDS force him over to the door and
handcuff him to it.)*

You may think it makes you look superior, but you

can take it from me that you're a dead ringer for a nun with a big one up her.

(THE SERGEANT punches KENNY in the gut for his blasphemy. KENNY doubles up, winded. FIONA looks alarmed.)

FIONA: Please, Sergeant. There's really no need -

SIMMONDS: I'm sorry, Mrs Carter, but I won't tolerate that sort of thing. I won't tolerate ladies being spoken to as if they're sluts from the gutter.

FIONA: It doesn't worry us, Sergeant. Really. We're used to it.

SIMMONDS: I'm sorry, Mrs Carter. You must let me handle this is in my own way.

SIMMONDS: *(to THE REMOVALIST)* Mrs Carter will tell you what to take. Give him a hand, Ross.

KENNY: *(agitated)* Hey. Just a minute. What's this in aid of?

SIMMONDS: *(tersely)* Shut up, Carter.

KENNY: *(to FIONA)* What? Are you leaving? Just because I give you the occasional odd shove?

SIMMONDS: *(louder)* I'm warning you, Carter.

KENNY: Fair's fair, Sergeant. That's my furniture. I paid for it.

SIMMONDS: *(grabbing him by the shirt-front)* Shut up.

KENNY: I only gave her a bit of a shove and by Christ she deserved it. She can't just walk out with my property.

SIMMONDS: *(releasing KENNY)* I'm led to believe that you don't even like this style of furniture, Carter.

KENNY: What's that got to do with it? I paid for it.

(He looks at FIONA and flares suddenly.)

Worked overtime to get it for the bitch and it was all she could do to spread the legs for me occasionally.

FIONA: *(flaring)* You've never worked overtime in your life. It was my money that paid for that furniture.

SIMMONDS: *(shaking KENNY)* I'm warning you, boy. I'll crack your bloody skull if I hear any more of that type of language.

REMOVALIST: *(impatient to get started)* That coffee table to go, Missus?

FIONA: *(calming)* Thank you.

(THE REMOVALIST motions ROSS, who bounds over and takes the coffee table out single-handed. THE REMOVALIST saunters after him.)

KENNY: *(to FIONA)* What? You're really leaving. You give a man a hell of a lot of warning don't you? Use me up when it's convenient and piss off when it suits you. Well, I'll tell you what. I'm no fool. These bastards can't come in here, beat me to a pulp and take me bloody furniture. *(Suddenly anxious)* Hey! What about Sophie?

FIONA: You can see Sophie.

KENNY: *(genuinely outraged)* See her! She's my bloody kid! You can't just take her away like that!

KATE: Well, you wouldn't think we'd leave her here do you? Just look at the way you live.

(She indicates the beer and sliced bread.)

KENNY: *(hurt, outraged)* There's nothin' wrong with the way I live, you bitch. *(To FIONA)* That little kid loves me. Follows me round like a little dog. We have a wrestle every night.

FIONA: *(guilty)* You can see her on the weekends.

KENNY: *(outraged)* I go to the footy on Saturday. You know that! You must be mad. How'd you think you're going to support yourself?

FIONA: I've got a job.

KENNY: By Christ. All I've done for you and this is me reward. If I hadn't looked after you in Munich you'd probably be still over there and peddling your twat to boot.

(THE SERGEANT punches KENNY in the gut. He is in command of the situation and enjoying it.

SIMMONDS: Didn't I tell you something about your language, Carter? Are you deaf or something?

KENNY: *(furious, winded, struggling)* You can't treat me like that, you bloody ape. I'll sue you for every penny you've got.

SIMMONDS: Well if that's the case I'd better give you something to complain about.

(SIMMONDS punches KENNY in the gut again as THE REMOVALIST and ROSS return.)

FIONA: *(alarmed at the violence)* Sergeant -

SIMMONDS: I'm sorry, Mrs Carter. I hate using violence on anyone, but there's one thing I won't tolerate and that's a man with no respect for womanhood.

REMOVALIST: Do the bastard good. What next, ladies?

FIONA: Oh er . . .

KATE: The cocktail cabinet, thank you.

KENNY: Hey. Just a minute. I use that.

KATE: What? To store your beer glasses.

KENNY: I'v got some of my stuff in there.

(THE SERGEANT moves to the cabinet and takes out some beer glasses.)

SIMMONDS: *(reading)* Croxton Park hotel. Are they selling their beer glasses these days, Carter?

KENNY: A mate gave 'em to me.

SIMMONDS: We'll book you for receiving stolen property then.
(He pulls out a tray.)
They don't make a habit of giving away their trays at the Croxton Park either. Not to my knowledge. Put 'em in the corner and hold 'em as evidence, Ross.

(ROSS puts the items in the corner and he and THE REMOVALIST take out the cabinet.)

KENNY: Fair go. Everyone pinches a few glasses.

SIMMONDS: You tell that to the magistrate.

KENNY: You better be sure of your facts.

SIMMONDS: *(pushing him hard against the door)* I what?

KENNY: That badge don't allow you to do anything you like.

SIMMONDS: *(pushing him heavily against the door again)* I'd keep quiet from now on if I were you, Carter. I could get you for assaulting an officer of the law, and you know what that would mean.

KENNY: I haven't touched yer.

SIMMONDS: We don't cuff people to the door for nothing, Carter. Constable Ross was only doing his duty and you bloody went berserk.

KENNY: *(indignant)* Went berserk? *(pointing to ROSS)* He's the one who went berserk. All I did was drag me feet.

SIMMONDS: If that was dragging your feet, I'd hate to see you punching someone up, Carter.

KENNY: Well Christ almighty. You come in here -

SIMMONDS: I'd keep quiet from now on if I were you, Carter. If you go up for assaulting an officer then Mrs Carter could have you barred from your kid.

KENNY: *(worried)* Bullshit.

SIMMONDS: It's no bullshit, Carter. Your wife could get a court order as easy as snapping her fingers. Undesirable influence.

KENNY: You think I'm a bloody fool, don't you? I'm going straight to a doctor to get a certificate about me bruises.

SIMMONDS: You'd be wasting your money. I haven't left a bruise in twenty-three years.

KENNY: I'll get Galbally.

SIMMONDS: Well, if you can afford three hundred dollars a day then I can't see why you're getting upset about your wife having some of the furniture.

KENNY: *(to KATE, after a pause)* Had a dream about you last night.

SIMMONDS: *(drawing his arm back in warning to KENNY)* Watch it, Carter.

KENNY: Dreamt you were makin' love to a gorilla.

KATE: *(coolly)* Very amusing.

KENNY: Full of remorse afterwards of course. Said you thought it was a police sergeant.

SIMMONDS: *(punching him in the gut)* All right, Carter. Apologise.

KENNY: Who to? You or the gorilla?

(SIMMONDS punches him again. FIONA is upset and goes to intervene but turns and goes out to the kitchen. THE REMOVALIST and ROSS return in time to witness this last act of violence.)

SIMMONDS: They don't bruise, Carter. You'd think they would, wouldn't you, but you can take my word for it. *(To ROSS)* That's something they didn't teach you in training school, eh?

REMOVALIST: Hate to interrupt mate, but I've got ten thousand dollars worth of machinery tickin' over out there in the drive.

SIMMONDS: *(irritated)* Have you left the bloody engine running?

REMOVALIST: Just a figure of speech.

SIMMONDS: *(tersely)* Take an armchair each. Right, Mrs Carter?

(FIONA, still in the kitchen, indicates that this is right.)

REMOVALIST: No need to get shirty with me, mate. You can punch up that bastard all you like, but I've got me job to do.

SIMMONDS: All right. Do your bloody job and take those chairs.

REMOVALIST: Nobody speaks to me like that, mate. *(To Ross)* We'll take the couch.

SIMMONDS: *(tersely to ROSS)* Take a bloody chair.

REMOVALIST: *(tersely to ROSS)* Grab the end of the couch.

SIMMONDS: *(loudly, to the bewildered ROSS)* Take the bloody chair.

REMOVALIST: *(cold fury)* The captain is master of the ship. Right?

SIMMONDS: Right what?

REMOVALIST: You can do what you like in here, mate, but once I'm in the back of me truck, my word is law. Right? I've been packing trucks for a long while and it's an art. You don't just throw the stuff in. Right? The logical thing to go next is the couch. Right?

SIMMONDS: *(exasperated)* Take the bloody couch, Ross.

REMOVALIST: *(condescending)* I don't want to seem like I'm making an issue of it, mate, but you get a bit fed up with the general public after a while because not many of them realise that there's a bit more to it than lugging furniture.

(ROSS and THE REMOVALIST take out the couch.)

SIMMONDS: *(turning on KENNY)* We haven't heard your apology to Mrs Mason yet, Carter.

KENNY: You're not likely to either.

SIMMONDS: *(menacing)* You just make trouble for yourself don't you?

KATE: Don't worry about it, Sergeant. I've had much worse than that from him before.

KENNY: Take off this handcuff and see whether you're such a big man then, copper.

SIMMONDS: I'd love to do that, Carter, because then I could let you have what you deserve and not hold anything back.

KENNY: Go on then. Undo the cuff.

SIMMONDS: You're really tempting me, boy.

KENNY: Go on; undo it.

SIMMONDS: You really want to have a go do you?

KENNY: Bloody oath.

KATE: Don't let him off, Sergeant. He's done a bit of boxing.

KENNY: Go on. Undo it.

SIMMONDS: I'd love to, Carter, but a good policeman never indulges himself.

KENNY: You're yellow. Come on. Uncuff me.

SIMMONDS: Listen, boy. I've won more fights than you've had breakfasts.

KENNY: You are yellow, you bastard.

SIMMONDS: I've already told you once that it'd only take one punch to land on Ross or I and you could forget your daughter. Is that what you want?

(KENNY scowls at SIMMONDS and yells out to FIONA.)

KENNY: I hope you realise what you're doing. I hope you realise that the minute you walk out of this door, that's it. I'm not havin' you back.

FIONA: *(coming out of the kitchen)* I don't intend to come back.

KENNY: You'd be hard put to find another man as good as me. I'll tell you that. *(Afterthought)* And if you have, you won't keep him long because good men are in short supply and they're not all as stupid as me.

FIONA: I haven't got another man.

KENNY: *(indicating KATE)* She's jealous. She's put you up to this because she's jealous.

FIONA: Kate didn't put me up to anything. I made up my own mind.

KENNY: *(scornfully)* Yeah.

FIONA: I did.

KENNY: Why didn't you have the guts to come and tell me yourself instead of letting your sister do the dirty work?

KATE: Fiona made up her own mind. She asked me along for moral support.

KENNY: *(sardonic)* Moral? Moral ain't the right word for you, you bloody trollop. The nymph of North Balwyn. Bangs like a buggered tappet.

(SIMMONDS moves towards him, but stops to watch KATE'S reaction.)

KATE: *(angry)* You make me sick.

KENNY: Well who are you to be handing out advice to Fiona? You'd be the greatest twat flasher in Melbourne bar none.

KATE: *(viciously)* You're a boorish, loud-mouthed, sickening little swine, and the sooner Fiona gets out of here the better. *(To the SERGEANT)* I think you can see why my sister has to leave.

KENNY: It's your bloody sister that tells me.

(KATE looks murderously at FIONA.)

KATE: *(to FIONA)* What have you been telling him?

FIONA: Nothing.

KENNY: *(to KATE)* What about your car salesman?
  Amongst others.

*(KATE looks murderously at FIONA. THE RE-
MOVALIST and ROSS re-enter. There is a pause.
THE REMOVALIST directs ROSS to take one of the
lounge chairs. He takes the other.)*

KATE: For God's sake. All this fuss about an affair.
  My God. This is the twentieth century isn't it? Anyone would think I was a nymphomaniac.

FIONA: *(to SIMMONDS)* She isn't.

KATE: *(sensing that her sister is gently sending her up)*
  My private life may not be spotless, Sergeant, but I
  want you to know that I'm very fond of my husband.

SIMMONDS: You don't have to offer me an explanation ,
  Mrs Mason.

KATE: *(looking murderously at FIONA)* They laugh
  at Ralph behind his back but he's a very fine man.
  He's provided a good life for me and my children
  and he's a fine man.

KENNY: If roots were hamburgers, you could feed a
  bloody army.

SIMMONDS: Watch it, Carter.

KENNY: I'm speaking from experience, Sergeant.
  (To KATE) Tell the Sergeant about our last Christmas
  barbecue.

KATE: Don't try and use that against me, you pig. I've
  told Fiona about that. She knows what happened.

KENNY: Come on. You tried to rip my bloody daks
  off until I told you to wake up to yourself.

KATE: I've told Fiona exactly what happened.

KENNY: Did you tell her what you did with me mate Billy McMaster later in the evening?

KATE: *(floored)* I . . .
(She turns to the SERGEANT)

KENNY: *(to the SERGEANT)* She just can't resist a well-packed fly.

(SIMMONDS slams KENNY against the door.)

SIMMONDS: That's enough from you, Carter.

KATE: *(to FIONA)* I was very drunk that night. I can't remember much about it.

FIONA: I wouldn't worry.

KATE: *(angrily)* And I don't care what he says. Your husband wasn't plying me with whisky for nothing.

KENNY: Bloody oath I wasn't. I was hoping you'd pass out.

KATE: *(angry)* You egged me on till I made a fool of myself, then deliberately humiliated me.
(Pause. She turns to FIONA.)
I've left the children with a baby sitter. If you don't mind I'll call a taxi.

SIMMONDS: *(narrowly)* Aren't you going to help your sister unpack, Mrs Mason?

KATE: No. I'm afraid I'll have to get home, Sergeant.

SIMMONDS: I see. Well don't call a taxi. I'll give you a lift. Ross and the removalist *(indicating the pair who have just returned)* can take care of the unpacking.

KATE: No. Thank you all the same, Sergeant. I'll call a taxi.

(She goes into the kitchen. SIMMONDS glares at her as she goes.)

KENNY: *(to FIONA)* Where are you moving into?

FIONA: A flat.

KENNY: And the lads here were going to help you shift in? I see.

SIMMONDS: *(menacing)* Shut up, Carter.

KENNY: Pity about Kate, Sergeant. You would've been in like Flynn.

(SIMMONDS slams KENNY against the door again.)

REMOVALIST: *(looking at his watch)* Excuse me, people. What's next on the agenda?

FIONA: *(hesitantly)* The television.

KENNY: *(explosively)* Now wait a minute!

SIMMONDS: *(yelling)* Shut up!

KENNY: At least you could leave us the bloody tube.

FIONA: Sophie watches Sesame Street.

KENNY: I watch every bloody thing.

SIMMONDS: *(to THE REMOVALIST)* Take it away.

(ROSS and THE REMOVALIST go towards it.)

KENNY: *(who has been watching the television intermittently)* Leave it on for a few more minutes. I want to see if the brother has a go at the wife.

(THE REMOVALIST looks at him as if to say: 'you must be joking', and unplugs it. He watches as ROSS winds up the lead and prepares to take it out.)

SIMMONDS: *(still snaky)* Did they teach you how to shift furniture in training Ross?

ROSS: *(sullen)* No.

SIMMONDS: *(to THE REMOVALIST, noting his

inclination to take things easy while ROSS does the work) I hope you're finding Ross satisfactory?

REMOVALIST: *(not picking the sarcasm)* I wouldn't hire the bastard.

SIMMONDS: Why not?

REMOVALIST: No experience. Lifts with his back. Jerks instead of easing. You've gotta know how to pace yourself. I can keep going all day.

SIMMONDS: Yes. I reckon you could.

REMOVALIST: Some bastards reckon that any fool can shift furniture, but I'll tell you what: I've been at it for years and I'm still learning.

SIMMONDS: Well. There you are, Ross. You're picking up a trade. That's what the force does for you.

REMOVALIST: It is a bloody trade, I'll tell you. I can pack a load that'll hold fast over the worst bullock track in Australia, and you don't learn that overnight, and you don't learn it out of no books, either.
(While this dialogue continues ROSS staggers towards the door carrying the television set.)
I was shiftin' some stuff for this big noise the other day and when I'd got it packed he wandered up for a bit of a look and said to me: 'That's really neat'. 'Just learned how to do it yesterday'. I said. 'Really', he said, and raised his eyebrows. 'You've picked it up remarkably quick.' Stupid prick. You wonder how some of those bastards make their money.
(He follows ROSS out.)

KENNY: *(to FIONA)* Are you going to leave me anything? You've taken me T.V. May as well have the fridge. And the washing machine. Take everything.

FIONA: There's a washing machine supplied.

KENNY: *(exploding)* You're not havin' the fridge.

FIONA: You only use it for beer.

KENNY: I do eat occasionally, you know.
(Pause.)
 You'd better let me see Sophie.

FIONA: *(flaring)* I told you you could see Sophie!

KENNY: At least once a week.

FIONA: All right!

KENNY: If I find you're setting yourself up for some
 man, I'll come and do the both of you and take
 Sophie.

FIONA: For Christ's sake. I am not setting myself up
 for anyone.

KENNY: I wouldn't put it past you. Sounds like you
 were all set up to pay off your obligations tonight.
 Which one was yours? The old fossil here? *(Indicating
 THE SERGEANT)* Looks like he couldn't raise the
 bus fare to Balwyn.

FIONA: *(angry)* That's how your mind works, doesn't
 it?

KENNY: Probably a twat flasher like your bloody
 sister.

*(SIMMONDS slams KENNY against the wall and
enjoys doing it.)*

KENNY: *(angry, to FIONA)* Call your bloody thug
 off.

*(FIONA, distressed by the violence and by KENNY'S
accusations, retreats into the kitchen.)*

KENNY: You're really a big man aren't you? Handcuff

a man to the door and beat him. I'll get you one day, copper.

(SIMMONDS glares at him. ROSS and THE REMOVALIST return.)

KENNY: *(in a softer voice)* How would you like to know something about me private life, Sergeant?

SIMMONDS: *(tight lipped)* I'm not interested, Carter.

KENNY: I came home last night after a long day's work and my sweet wife, as sometimes happens, was very friendly. She came five times in the one grapple, Sergeant. *(Yelling in the SERGEANT'S face)* And the next bloody day she's leavin' me!

(THE SERGEANT goes berserk. It is as if KENNY'S words have found the trigger to switch him from controlled to uncontrolled violence. He beats KENNY about the face. ROSS is alarmed. KENNY is shaken. THE REMOVALIST watches with interest. The two women come out of the kitchen in time to see the latter part of the violence and are too shocked to intervene.)

KENNY: You've done your dough now, copper. That'll show up for sure. Do it again and really get yourself in the shit. Come on. Do it again. *(To FIONA)* Why don't you tell the Sergeant yourself? I might be a beer-swilling slob but you squeal like a stuck pig for me in bed. Don't you? Go on. Tell the bastard. Tell him how you can't get enough of it sometimes.

(SIMMONDS knees him in the gut. He breathes heavily. His voice is loud and jagged with emotion.)

SIMMONDS: What d'you think that proves, Carter? D'you think that's the test of a man? D'you think that's the test? Self control is the test of manhood, Carter. Self bloody control. My wife had twenty -

seven kidney fits having our son, Carter. Bloody near died. Both of them. I couldn't go near her for five bloody years after that because she wasn't allowed to get pregnant again. *(Roaring)* There's your manhood for you, Carter. Self bloody control!

(There is a pause. Everyone is shocked at THE SERGEANT'S odd outburst. FIONA is dumbstruck, but KATE moves towards SIMMONDS to calm him. ROSS and THE REMOVALIST take the refrigerator out.)

KATE: Twenty-seven kidney fits. That's terrible.

SIMMONDS: *(breathing heavily)* Yes. We gave her up at one stage.

KATE: Your ... your boy. He was all right?

SIMMONDS: Fit as a fiddle. Training with Preston next year.

KATE: But it ... er ... meant you couldn't have any more?

SIMMONDS: We had another one. A daughter. Got five kids of her own now. One a year.

KATE: Your wife went ahead and risked it?

SIMMONDS: The doctors said she shouldn't but she came through with flying colours.

KATE: That's marvellous.

SIMMONDS: Yes. It turned out pretty well in the end, but you never know at the time. Have you got any kiddies yourself?

KATE: Yes. The eldest started third grade this year.

SIMMONDS: What school?

KATE: Grammar.

SIMMONDS: Melbourne?

KATE: Geelong.

SIMMONDS: Fine school. I'd like a penny for every notable that's been educated there. I wanted my boy to go to a private school but I couldn't see my way clear on a policeman's salary.

KATE: Yes. The costs are scandalous these days. It's not helping our budget I can tell you.

SIMMONDS: It's not so bad if your salary's high. Educational expenses are tax deductible.

KATE: *(feigning ignorance)* Are they? That probably explains why we're still solvent.

(THE SERGEANT looks narrowly at KATE. KENNY breathes heavily on the floor, scared for the first time by THE SERGEANT'S violence. ROSS and THE REMOVALIST return.)

REMOVALIST: Anything else to go?

FIONA: The cot from Sophie's room.

KENNY: *(mildly, to FIONA)* What about when she visits me?

SIMMONDS: *(hoisting KENNY to his feet and speaking with menace)* I don't think we want to hear your voice any more, Carter, in fact I'm sure of it, in fact if I hear it one more time I'll split your skull and be damned to Galbally. Get me!

(KENNY, genuinely afraid, doesn't say a word.)

SIMMONDS: *(to ROSS)* Get the cot.

FIONA: No, actually it can stay here. Kate's going to give me her old cot. I'd forgotten.

KATE: Yes. I'm hoping I won't need it any more.

SIMMONDS: *(flatly)* Please yourself.

FIONA: *(to the men)* Perhaps if you could take the double bed from our bedroom.

(ROSS and THE REMOVALIST move offstage.)

KATE: *(to FIONA)* Well that . . . er . . . taxi should be here any minute. I'm sorry I couldn't help you shift in.

(FIONA shrugs.)

SIMMONDS: How many children have you got altogether, Mrs Mason?

KATE: Three
(Pause. THE SERGEANT keeps looking at her.)
Mark's the eldest. He's eight. Dionne is six and Anthony's five.

SIMMONDS: Well spaced.

KATE: Too well spaced, but they're all at school now, thank God.

SIMMONDS: Gives you more spare time, I suppose.

KATE: Yes. It does give me a bit more breathing space.

SIMMONDS: *(flatly)* I hope you're using it to good advantage.

KATE: Yes. I'm able to get out and about a bit these days.

SIMMONDS: You're doing a bit of shopping, I take it?

KATE: That's right.

SIMMONDS: For cars?

(There is an awkward pause. ROSS and THE

REMOVALIST walk through with the bed.)

KATE: *(stiffly)* Not really.

SIMMONDS: I was wondering how you met your friend?

KATE: What friend?

SIMMONDS: Your car salesman friend.

KATE: *(embarrassed)* Oh. Eric. Oh. He isn't really a car salesman in that sense. He's the marketing manager of one of our largest car manufacturers.

SIMMONDS: That's a very responsible position.

KATE: Yes. It is.

SIMMONDS: I wouldn't have thought that a man in a position like that would have very much spare time.

KATE: No. He's kept very busy.

SIMMONDS: I wouldn't have thought he'd have very much spare time at all.
(Pause.)
Is he married?

KATE: *(wary)* Eric?

SIMMONDS: Mmm.

KATE: *(defensive)* Yes. He is.

SIMMONDS: Children I suppose?

KATE: *(defensive)* Yes. Three boys.

SIMMONDS: Private schooling I suppose?

KATE: As a matter of fact, yes. His eldest's at Uni now studying law.

SIMMONDS: Law, eh?

KATE: He's doing very well.

SIMMONDS: I bet he is. It's much easier studying law than administering it.
(Pause.)
Do his children know he's an adulterer?

KATE: *(shocked)* If you don't mind!

SIMMONDS: Do your children know you're an adulterer?

FIONA: Sergeant! I don't think -

SIMMONDS: *(hard edge in voice, indicating KENNY)*
I can understand the likes of this bastard behaving like that. But I can't understand it from people in responsible positions, Mrs Mason. I can't understand that at all.

KATE: I don't think my private life is any of your business, Sergeant.

SIMMONDS: I didn't say it was, Mrs Mason. I am merely expressing an opinion.

(ROSS and THE REMOVALIST enter.)

KATE: *(icy)* I'm not interested in your opinion, Sergeant.

SIMMONDS: *(loudly)* I couldn't care less whether you are interested in my opinion or not, Mrs Mason. I am certainly entitled to express it. In my opinion people in responsible positions have a duty to ensure that their behaviour is beyond reproach. Does your husband know about this?

KATE: If you don't mind, I think I'll wait for my taxi outside.

SIMMONDS: *(loudly)* A position of privilege carries certain responsibilities, Mrs Mason. A man who occupies a position of leadership in industry should not abuse that responsibility. I hope he doesn't work for Ford. I drive a Ford.

KATE: *(leaving)* Excuse me.

SIMMONDS: *(following her and talking loudly)* Some of you people think you can do anything. Do you ever   spare a thought for your husband? Working to give you and your children a better life. It can't be much fun peering into other people's mouths, fiddling with their bloody molars, half of them with bad bloody breath. Why don't you try being grateful for a change instead of cheating on him behind his back with a man who's got a family of his own?

(The voices become indistinct offstage as SIMMONDS systematically humiliates her. FIONA looks at KENNY and the other two men and follows THE SERGEANT and KATE offstage, hoping, presumably to aid her sister.)

REMOVALIST: *(to ROSS)* What goes next?

ROSS: *(to KENNY)* What goes next?

KENNY: *(sharply)* How in the hell would I know, you great Burke?

ROSS: *(hurt, angry)* I was only asking.

(Pause.)

REMOVALIST: *(insistently)* What goes next?

ROSS: I'll . . . er . . . go outside and ask.

(ROSS leaves.)

KENNY: Do us a favour will you?

REMOVALIST: Me business is shiftin' furniture, mate. Not doin' favours.

KENNY: Just do us one small favour.

REMOVALIST: What?

KENNY: Ring the cops.

REMOVALIST: *(indicating offstage)* They do happen to be the cops, you know.

KENNY: Ring Russell Street.

REMOVALIST: Why?

KENNY: That sergeant's going to beat shit outa me. He's as mad as a bloody snake.

REMOVALIST: What makes you think that?

KENNY: You saw the bastard. He's off his nut.

REMOVALIST: You provoked him.

KENNY: *(incredulous)* Provoked him? I didn't provoke him just then, did I?

REMOVALIST: I reckon she's a bloody trollop too.

KENNY: Yeah, but you don't go round screamin' at her. Do you?

REMOVALIST: Yeah, but I'm not a cop.

KENNY: That's not the bloody point.

REMOVALIST: *(thinking)* Yeah, well what about you? You screamed at her before.

KENNY: *(getting desperate)* Yeah, but I had good cause.

REMOVALIST: Well maybe he thinks he had good cause.

KENNY: Look, for Christ's sake be a good bloke and ring Russell Street.

REMOVALIST: You must be mad. Do you think they'd come down and collar their own mates?

KENNY: All right then. Will you ring some of my

mates as well?

REMOVALIST: How many bloody phone calls do you want me to make?

KENNY: It won't take you a minute.

REMOVALIST: *(shakes his head)* I can't afford to get involved, mate. I've got ten thousand dollars worth of equipment tickin' over out there in the drive.

KENNY: Jesus! It wouldn't take much effort.

REMOVALIST: Sorry, mate. I ve got a pretty simple philosophy. If there's work I work, and if nobody interferes with me then I don't interfere with nobody.

KENNY: *(agitated)* For Christ's sake -

REMOVALIST: I mind me own business if other people mind theirs, and that's the way I play the game. Get me?

(ROSS comes back inside. He has been abused by SIMMONDS and is irritated and angry.)

REMOVALIST: *(to ROSS)* What else has got to go?

ROSS: *(surly)* I don't know.

REMOVALIST: Didn't you ask someone?

ROSS: *(irritated)* They're still shouting at each other.

REMOVALIST: Look. I've got ten thousand dollars worth of machinery tickin' over out there.

ROSS: *(angry)* Shut up!

REMOVALIST: That's all right about you. It's my living isn't it?

ROSS: Shut up!

REMOVALIST: What? Am I supposed to sit here while your boss argues sin and damnation with the ladies?

ROSS: *(sharply)* Just shut up. *(To KENNY)* Look you. What else has got to go?

KENNY: *(looks at him in amazement)* How would I know?

ROSS: You're her bloody husband.

KENNY: I only found out she was leavin' tonight!

(ROSS moves offstage in a fury.)

ROSS: *(off)* Would she want this dresser in the bedroom?

KENNY: *(irritated)* Jesus, mate!

ROSS: *(reappearing)* Well, does she like it?

KENNY: *(sarcastic)* I'm sorry Constable, but my wife and I didn't spend much time discussing her innermost feelings for the dresser. It's something we've been meaning to do for a long time, but we just keep putting it off. D'you think that could have something to do with the failure of our marriage?

ROSS: *(nervy and agitated)* Look. I haven't hit you, Carter. I haven't hit you so there's no need to get funny with me. This gentleman can't be expected to hang around all day.

REMOVALIST: *(sagely)* That's right, fella. I've got ten thousand dollars worth of machinery tickin' over out there.

KENNY: If I hear you say that once again mate, I'll piss in your radiator and shit in your gearbox.

REMOVALIST: *(defensively)* That's all right for you. You wage-earners don't realise that time is money and money is time.

ROSS: I thought you were being paid by the hour.

REMOVALIST: *(touchy)* That's not the point. That's not the point at all. If I can get this job wrapped up early I might be able to pick up a late job before I knock off.

ROSS: All right then. Take the bloody dresser.

REMOVALIST: On who's authority?

ROSS: On my authority.

REMOVALIST: *(sitting down and taking out a smoke)* I want to get movin'. Fair enough. But I'm not going off half cocked.

ROSS: Go to buggery then.

(ROSS sits down. SIMMONDS strides back in and sees the two of them sitting around.)

SIMMONDS: *(loudly)* What's all this? A bloody smoko?

REMOVALIST: If one knew what item one was dealing with next one might bloody well get on with it.

SIMMONDS: *(walking offstage)* Take this dresser in here! *(Coming back)* Why didn't you use your bloody initiative, Ross?

ROSS: *(protesting)* I did.

REMOVALIST: *(to SIMMONDS)* How d'you know the dresser's got to go?

SIMMONDS: *(ominously)* Take the bloody dresser!

(They move off to get the dresser. SIMMONDS calls after ROSS.)

SIMMONDS: Why couldn't you have done that?

ROSS: *(turning, in protest)* I did. I told him to take the dresser.

SIMMONDS: Then why didn't you boot him up the arse. Now go on. Jump to it!

(ROSS and THE REMOVALIST move off. FIONA returns from outside and stands there hesitantly. SIMMONDS stands looking at her.)

FIONA: Perhaps the dresser in the bedroom could go next.

SIMMONDS: They're getting it.

KENNY: *(to FIONA)* You haven't even thought this all out, have you?

FIONA: *(defensively)* Yes I have.

KENNY: *(with a sudden thought)* Is your mother going to give you money?

FIONA: *(edgy)* No.

KENNY: *(pressing)* She's giving you money, isn't she?

FIONA: She gave me the deposit on the flat. That's all!

KENNY: How in the hell do you think you're going to live on your salary?

FIONA: You'll be paying me something.

KENNY: *(indignant)* Like hell I will! You're the one who's leavin' me. I don't have to pay a thing!

SIMMONDS: You're obliged to contribute to the upkeep of your daughter, Carter.

KENNY: *(indignant)* Come off it. She's leavin' me. Why should I pay? Her mother's filthy rich.

SIMMONDS: You're obliged to pay for the upkeep of your daughter, Carter.

KENNY: *(outraged)* But she's walkin' out on me!

SIMMONDS: You beat her up! She's got a medical certificate!

KENNY: *(exasperated)* Christ! What's the bloody world comin' to! In the old days if a man didn't give his wife a thrashing every week or so she wouldn't respect him. Nowadays you give 'em a love pat and they shoot through on you.

SIMMONDS: *(to FIONA)* I'm sorry I lost my temper with your sister, Mrs Carter.

FIONA: *(embarrassed)* You did make her quite upset.

SIMMONDS: Yes. I'm a man of strong convictions, I'm afraid.

FIONA: I don't really think there was any need to speak to her like that.

SIMMONDS: Don't you think there's a place for a little bit of honesty in the world, Mrs Carter?

FIONA: Yes, but if you saw her husband Ralph you might understand.

(FIONA grins at KENNY, but he is in no mood to respond to their long-standing private joke. She realises the the valuable aspects of her relationship with KENNY are no longer available to her and feels vulnerable.)

SIMMONDS: I'll still help you move that furniture into the flat if you'd like me to, Mrs Carter.

(KENNY glares at SIMMONDS. He knows what SIMMONDS is about. SIMMONDS knows that KENNY knows and is enjoying FIONA'S confusion and KENNY'S anger.)

FIONA: Well . . . er . . . *(looking at KENNY)*
Look. don't bother, Sergeant. It should be all right.

SIMMONDS: Is your flat on the ground floor, Mrs

Carter?

FIONA: No, it's a first floor flat.

SIMMONDS: Yes, well, you'll need another man. Won't you?

KENNY: Lay off her, copper.

SIMMONDS: You'll have to get used to the fact that your wife will need assistance from other men from time to time, Carter.

KENNY: *(to FIONA, flaring)* You think this's going to be one great big ball, don't you? You're in for a bloody great shock. One in every three men is a premature ejaculator. Did you sister ever tell you that? One in three's got a bloody weak back. You ask her! You've been dying to try it all out for years, haven't you? Well don't come crawlin' back to me. That's all I'm sayin'. Don't come crawlin' back to me!

FIONA: *(flaring)* For God's sake! The thing I'm looking forward to most is a rest!

(ROSS and THE REMOVALIST enter again.)

REMOVALIST: What's next?

FIONA: *(still shaken)* If you could take the cupboard in the baby's room that would just about be it.

(THE REMOVALIST nods. He and ROSS move off. KATE enters, still furious.)

KATE: *(to FIONA)* The taxi's arrived, Fiona. Do you want to come with me?

FIONA: *(confused)* Where to?

KATE: To the flat.

SIMMONDS: *(to KATE)* You can go home, Mrs Mason. I'll help Mrs Carter and the removalist.

KATE: *(teeth clenched)* Oh no you won't. You won't go near that flat tonight or any other night. For all your moralising you're nothing but a pervert, Sergeant. I know your type. I saw the look on your face when you were fondling Fiona's thigh down at the station.

SIMMONDS: *(livid)* Get out!

KATE: Don't threaten me!

SIMMONDS: *(loud)* Get outside!

KATE: What will you do if I don't? Chain me to the bloody door and rape me?

SIMMONDS: *(advancing on her)* Get outside!

KATE: Tell us all what happened down at the station, Sergeant. Tell us!

(THE REMOVALIST and ROSS re-enter carrying the cupboard.)

REMOVALIST: *(looking at his watch)* This is the last thing, then?

SIMMONDS: *(to KATE, a little hysterical himself)* You're a liar, woman. A bloody liar and you're not fooling anyone.
(Pause.)
The truth of the matter is that you tried you best to seduce us from the word go. *(Pointing to ROSS)* A young boy straight out of training school. Could've scarred him for life!

REMOVALIST: *(to FIONA)* This is the last item then?

(FIONA nods.)

KATE: *(to the REMOVALIST)* Can you find another man at short notice, removalist?

REMOVALIST: Another man to help unload?

(KATE nods.)

REMOVALIST: Well, that's a bit tricky, missus. I was contracted out under the understanding that another man would be supplied by the hirer.

FIONA: *(agitated)* I'll help.

REMOVALIST: It's not the sort of work for a lady, love.

KATE: *(tight-lipped)* Could you find another man?

REMOVALIST: Well, probably. Yes. It'll cost you double time though.

KATE: I don't care what it will cost. Have you got the address?

REMOVALIST: Indeed I have, Ma'am.

(KATE nods and takes FIONA'S arm. She goes to move outside. FIONA turns to KENNY, but he has already started to talk to SIMMONDS.)

KENNY: Look, they've got all the furniture. You can let me go now.

FIONA: *(to KENNY)* Look, I'll get in touch tomorrow about Sophie.

KENNY: Could you tell him to let me go now?

FIONA: Could you let him off the handcuffs now, Sergeant?

SIMMONDS: Mr Carter was not handcuffed for your convenience, Mrs Carter. Mr Carter is being detained pending arrest for offensive behaviour.

FIONA: I'm not intending to press charges against him.

SIMMONDS: *(with relish)* I'm afraid the matter is out of your hands, Mrs Carter. The offences have

been committed against myself and Constable
Ross.

KATE: *(sharply)* Are you coming, Fiona? The taxi
won't wait around all day.

KENNY: He's going to beat shit out of me, Fiona.

KATE: *(sharply)* Don't be so ridiculous!

*(KATE drags a bewildered FIONA out to the taxi.
ROSS returns. There is a pause.)*

SIMMONDS: *(ominously)* Why would we beat shit
out of you, Carter?
*(SIMMONDS walks up to him, pushes his head against
the door and looks into his eyes.)*
Why would we do that? *(To ROSS)* Can you think
of any reason why we'd do that, Ross?

ROSS: *(sullen)* No.

SIMMONDS: What's wrong with you, Ross?

ROSS: *(sullen)* Nothing.

SIMMONDS: You've been stomping around like a
constipated bear since we arrived, Ross. If you've
got something to say then get it off your chest.
Have you got something to say?

ROSS: *(sullen)* No.

SIMMONDS: I'll tell you what, Ross; if your attitude
doesn't show a marked improvement I'm going to
give you a rocket in your first report. *(Loudly)* If
you've got a chip on your shoulder then knock it
off, Ross, and knock it off right now or I'll turn
it into a bloody great log. Now knock it off, Ross.
(Bellowing) Knock it off. Get me?
(ROSS sulks. There is a long pause.)
What d'you think of Ross's potential, Carter?
Think he's going to make a good cop? Got what it

takes?
(KENNY remains silent.)

Well. What d'you think?

KENNY: *(quietly)* Look, how about undoing these cuffs.

SIMMONDS: I asked you a question, Carter. Do you think Ross's.going to be any great shakes as a policeman?

KENNY: I've got me doubts.

SIMMONDS: So have I. What d'you think are his main weaknesses?

KENNY: Bit hard to know where to start.

SIMMONDS: Take your time.

KENNY: *(trying to pass it off)* It's a bit hard to say on the spur of the moment.

SIMMONDS: *(feigning irritation)* I only want an opinion, Carter. I'm not asking for your balls, now am I? What do you think it is that Ross is lacking?

KENNY: He seems a bit slow up top.

SIMMONDS: Initiative, perhaps. Do you think he's lacking in initiative?

KENNY: Yeah. I had noticed that.

SIMMONDS: *(to ROSS)* Do you think we should beat the shit out of this bastard, Ross?
(ROSS doesn't answer.)
    (loud) For Christ's sake, Ross. Show a bit of initiative. Should we beat the shit out of this bastard?

ROSS: *(loud)* No!

(SIMMONDS gives a mock sigh of relief at ROSS'S display of initiative.)

SIMMONDS: Very good, Ross.
(Without warning SIMMONDS hits CARTER savagely in the groin with his knee. KENNY doubles up in pain.)
    I think you're right, Ross. We shouldn't beat him up. He's not worth the effort.
(He adjusts his hat.)
    Get your handcuffs.
(ROSS unlocks KENNY, avoiding his eye.)
    All right, Ross. Let's go.

(They turn to go. As they walk towards the door, KENNY raises himself on his elbow and yells venomously after SIMMONDS.)

KENNY: *(still in pain)* You dead cunt!

SIMMONDS: We don't want any more trouble from you, Carter.

KENNY: I'll get you one day, boy. I'll get you, you animal. I've got a lot of mates.

SIMMONDS: Think yourself lucky I didn't charge you, Carter. Don't push your luck.

KENNY: Get out! Go on. Get out, you animal. You'll step out of your house one dark night and you'll get it, boy. Kenny Carter doesn't forget somethin' like this. Now piss off to your police station and crawl back into the woodwork!

SIMMONDS: *(coolly, after a pause)* Book him, Ross. Abusive and threatening language.
(ROSS hesitates.)
    Book him!

(ROSS walks over towards KENNY who picks up a chair and threatens him.)

KENNY: *(menacing)* Don't you come any closer, shithead!

ROSS: I'm placing you under arrest for abusive and

threatening language, Carter. I must warn you -

KENNY: *(advancing on him)* Get out of my house you bloody great half-wit. You've had your fun, now get out!

ROSS: *(backing away)* I would advise you that any attempt -

SIMMONDS: Add deliberate obstruction and menacing behaviour, Ross.

ROSS: In addition to the earlier charges I am . . . *(backing away as KENNY advances)* charging you with deliberate -

KENNY: *(steamed up and sensing ROSS'S fear)* Do you think that uniform makes you a big man or something? Eh? Christ. A hundred bloody uniforms wouldn't do anything for you, boy. You're the bloody dregs. There's no bloody doubt about it. I've seen some cowardly fuckwits hiding behind their uniforms in my time but without a doubt you're the bottom of the bloody barrel.

(ROSS can take it no longer. He goes temporarily berserk and launches himself at KENNY who is taken by surprise and drops the chair. ROSS knocks him to the floor, punches him and starts to bash his head against the floor. KENNY breaks free and backs away in terror at the ferocity of ROSS'S attack. He breaks away and moves out into the kitchen, which is offstage. ROSS chases him. There are crashes and blows offstage. SIMMONDS grins to himself. There is silence, and after a pause ROSS comes back. He is panting and has blood on his face.)

SIMMONDS: Did you let him get away?
(ROSS is out of breath. He seems dazed.)
    Did you let him get away?

(ROSS is frightened. He looks at SIMMONDS)

ROSS: *(softly, hoarse)* I've killed the bastard, Serg.

SIMMONDS: *(amused)* Come on, Ross. Haven't you ever knocked a man out before?

ROSS: *(frightened)* I think I've killed him.

SIMMONDS: You better not have bruised him, boy. I hope it was a nice clean punch on the chin.

ROSS: *(frightened)* No, look I really think I killed him.

SIMMONDS: Yes, well I'm afraid I'm going to have to report this incident to cover myself in case anything does blow up, but if you hit him on the chin you should be right.

ROSS: I lost control, Serg. I just lost control.

SIMMONDS: Control is something you're going to have to learn, boy. Control is the essence of the law.

ROSS: I just couldn't stop myself.

SIMMONDS: Whenever you hit a man, Ross, you should know exactly how hard you're going to hit him a full minute before you land the blow. That's a good little rule to remember.

ROSS: *(agitated)* Christ, Serg. What's going to happen to me?

SIMMONDS: Don't worry, boy. I've got to hand in a report but I'll word it as gently as I can. I'll say that while I thought you used excessive force to detain the prisoner, it is my opinion that this mistake was almost entirely due to inexperience and certainly not to any defect of personality or the like. It'll be a good chance to have a bit of a dig at the police school. I'll point out how inadequately they prepare recruits for the reality of their vocation.

ROSS: *(loud)* Look, for Christ's sake, Serg. I killed him. I really killed him!

SIMMONDS: Come on, Ross. The human being is a hell of a lot tougher than most people give him credit for. Most recruits get in a panic after their first K.O.

ROSS: *(loud)* Go in there and have a look!

SIMMONDS: I've thrown a man down a flight of concrete steps, Ross, and seen him land on his bloody head. Ten minutes later he got up and walked away. Pretty neanderthal-looking specimen admittedly, but there you are. The only thing you've got to worry about is that Carter might rake up a bit of money and follow this through but unless they're filthy rich they usually think twice about that one when they cool down.

ROSS: For Christ's sake go in there and have a look, Serg!

(SIMMONDS shrugs and walks into the kitchen. He comes back with a worried look on his face.)

SIMMONDS: *(angry)* What'd you do to him?

ROSS: *(scared)* Is he dead?

SIMMONDS: He's pretty bloody white. What in the hell did you do to him?

ROSS: *(agitated)* I lost control.

SIMMONDS: What in the hell did you do? Hit him when he was down?

ROSS: No.

SIMMONDS: You didn't kick him, did you? You didn't kick him in the head?

ROSS: No. I never kicked.

SIMMONDS: But you hit him when he was down, didn't you?

ROSS: I might have. I lost control.

SIMMONDS: You idiot, Ross. You never hit a head that hasn't got some freedom of movement. For Christ's sake. Don't you know anything?

ROSS: Is he dead?

SIMMONDS: Well, he's looking pretty white.

ROSS: Why didn't you feel his pulse?

SIMMONDS: Because I came out to find out what you did to him.

ROSS: Well for Christ's sake go and feel his pulse.

SIMMONDS: Don't order me around, boy.

ROSS: Go and feel his pulse.

SIMMONDS: I tell you what, Ross. You'll go if he's dead. I can't help you much if he's dead.

ROSS: *(wildly)* We could make it look like he committed suicide.

SIMMONDS: *(talking fast and sternly)* What? Why in the hell would we say that? To protect you? Drag myself in to protect you? Do you think we'd get away - look, his wife, the sister, the removalist - do you honestly think we'd get away with a thing like that? Headquarters may be pretty dense but I tell you what, I'm not sticking my neck out to cover up for your mistakes, Ross - your bloody lack of control. What's the training school sending out these days? Punchies? Too much adrenalin or something?

ROSS: *(hysterical)* They'd believe it, Serg. He's had a hell of a day. You'd have to admit that. Wife walks out on him without a word of warning. Takes his television and his fridge. Just imagine if it happened to you, Serg. Just imagine. It'd hit you right in the gut, wouldn't it? I mean to say, he had no bloody warning, the poor bastard. Did the right thing by his wife in bed the night before, loves his daughter, and we didn't even let him see the end of the movie he was watchin'. I tell you he's had a bad day. If I was him I'd be thinkin' of the best way to kick it right now!

SIMMONDS: *(pushing him away, starting to show signs of panic himself)* You're mad Ross. You've gone right off. Do you think anyone commits suicide by beating himself to death? Gets all depressed and starts swingin' uppercuts at himself? You're in the shit I'm afraid, Ross. There's no two ways about it and it isn't going to help you one little bit to lose your head and come up with crazy stuff like that. You're in real strife, boy, and I'm afraid -

ROSS: *(starts foraging around in the cupboard)* We could hang him. Find a bit of rope and make it look as if he bloody hung himself.

SIMMONDS: *(fast and agitated)* Don't be so bloody stupid. What about the bruises and the blood? How're you going to explain that? I've been in the force twenty-three years now, Ross, and I know what you can get away with and what you can't; and I'm telling you for sure - you won't get away with a stunt like that. Not a hope in high heaven. You've gone too far, boy, and I'm afraid you're going to have to face the consequences.

ROSS: *(wildly, loud)* I'll say that you did it!

SIMMONDS: *(staggered)* You'll what?

ROSS: *(wildly)* I'll say that you did it!

SIMMONDS: *(aghast)* You can't lie about a thing like this, Ross!

ROSS: You were the one who was hitting him. They all

saw that. They'll believe me for sure.

SIMMONDS: *(anxious)* They all saw that I was in control, Ross. That's what they all saw. I know how hard to hit a man. That's what they all saw.

ROSS: I'll say that as soon as they left you went berserk and killed him.

SIMMONDS: *(anxious)* No, Ross. I'm in control and people know it. They can call me all kinds of bastard but they know I'm always in control, Ross. That's my strength Ross, and that's been my strength for years and nobody's going to believe otherwise because that's the work of a raw young hot-head if ever I saw it and other people are going to see it that way too Ross whether you like it or not, and that's something you're going to have to face up to instead of trying to shift the blame to an area where it doesn't rightly belong and where nobody in their right senses would ever see it as belonging. I think you must be mad to think that anyone would - I think you'd best come down to the main station and confess straight away before you go getting yourself into real trouble.

ROSS: *(wildly)* No, bugger you. I'm going to lie. I'm really going to turn it on. I'm going to lie and lie and lie and lie. You wait and see. I'm sorry Serg but I'm scared. I'm shit scared.

SIMMONDS: *(hysterical)* For Christ's sake don't get hysterical. Pull yourself together man!

ROSS: I'm sorry Serg but I'm scared. Shit scared.

SIMMONDS: Well getting hysterical isn't going to help!

ROSS: They'll lock us up Serg! They'll lock us up for life!

SIMMONDS: They won't lock me up! I've got nothing

to do with it!

ROSS: They won't put us in for life, will they Serg?
They never put us cops away for as long as ordinary
blokes, do they? *(Remembers)* Ooo Jesus! Yes they
do. Remember those two guys who knocked off
the T.A.B.? I'm sorry Serg, but I'm going to lie.
After all, you were in charge.

SIMMONDS: *(exploding)* I didn't tell you to kill him,
Ross. I didn't tell you to kill him!

ROSS: I'm no killer. I didn't join the force to kill
people. *(Sudden idea)* Let's leave a suicide note and
blast his head off with a shotgun. They won't find
the bruises then.

SIMMONDS: *(yelling)* Shut up, you crazy bastard!

*(KENNY, battered and bleeding, crawls into the room
unseen and hoists himself onto one of the few remaining
chairs, lighting himself a cigarette and taking a deep draw.)*

ROSS: *(yelling back)* Well good God, wouldn't you be
depressed if your wife just walked out on you without
a word of warning? If we blow his head off with a
shotgun I won't have to lie about who killed him!

SIMMONDS: For Christ's sake shut up and pull yourself
together! It isn't going to do you any good to lie.
They'll find bloodstains on your uniform and things
like that. The best thing you could do would be to
own up. The worst you'll face is manslaughter - officer
in the course of his duty - and I wouldn't mind betting
you'll get off on the grounds of inexperience. Yes.
Loss of control due to inexperience. I'll testify to
your inexperience. They probably won't let you stay
in the force but if you play your cards right you'll
get your full superannuation entitlements on the grounds
of psychological instability, and they can't take that
away from you, boy, even if you get another job, because

being unsuited to the force doesn't mean you're not
suited to something else and they -

ROSS: *(shouts)* Don't crap!

SIMMONDS: It's no crap! There's a young bloke over
Clifton Hill -

ROSS: That was a different case altogether.

SIMMONDS: Almost exactly the same!

ROSS: It was nothing like it!

SIMMONDS: Same sort of thing exactly!

ROSS: Don't crap!

*(There is a pause. ROSS and SIMMONDS stare
belligerently at each other. KENNY takes the cigarette
out of his mouth and exhales. They look around. They
look at each other.)*

KENNY: *(speaking with difficulty)* Did you two pricks
think you did me?

*(ROSS'S relief is profound. He runs over to KENNY
and practically kisses him.)*

ROSS: Thank Christ! I thought you were gone, boy.
Jesus am I glad to see you. Shit. Was I worried?
Was I ever. *(Apologetic)* Dunno what happened to
me in there, Carter. Went berserk! No other word
for it! Went right off me head.
(Pause.)
Jesus, was I worried. I tell you what - feel my forehead -
talk about sweat. I was in a bad way.

SIMMONDS: You bloody idiot, Ross!

ROSS: *(defensively)* You thought he was gone too! You
went in there.

SIMMONDS: You're a bloody idiot, Ross!

KENNY: Get me a bloody quack!

ROSS: You on the phone?

(KENNY shakes his head.)

KENNY: There's one down a couple of blocks.

ROSS: Which way?
(KENNY points. ROSS goes to leave. SIMMONDS restrains him.)
 I'm going to get a doctor!

SIMMONDS: Just hold it a minute!

ROSS: *(urgently)* He's got to get to a doctor!

SIMMONDS: He's not all that bad!

KENNY: Look, fair's fair. Get me a doctor.

SIMMONDS: You're all right. Just a bit of bruising.

KENNY: More than a bit of bruising, mate. Something's buggered in me eye.

ROSS: In your eye? Shit I hope it's not something serious. Shit I'm sorry mate. We better get you to a doctor quick smart.

(He moves over to KENNY to examine the eye. SIMMONDS moves across and pushes ROSS aside.)

SIMMONDS: Which eye?

KENNY: The left one.

SIMMONDS: *(looking at it)* Put your hand over your right eye.
(KENNY does so.)
 Can you see anything?

KENNY: No.

(SIMMONDS swings a punch at KENNY that stops just short of his face. KENNY, hand still over his right eye,

reels backward in anticipation of the blow. He nearly topples off his chair.)

SIMMONDS: You'll have to get up earlier in the morning than that to catch me out, Carter.

KENNY: *(defensively)* I can see a little bit out of it, but something's still buggered in there. Me eyeball feels like it's pressing against me skull. Something's buggered!

SIMMONDS: Mild concussion, Carter. Do you feel nauseous?

KENNY: Bloody oath.

SIMMONDS: Yes. You'll have a hell of a head tomorrow. No worse than a bad hangover, though.

KENNY: There's somethin' wrong in me gut too.

ROSS: *(anxious)* Shit. Whereabouts? Where's it hurt?

KENNY: *(pointing to his side)* In there.

ROSS: Jesus, Serg. We better get him to a doctor.

KENNY: Yeah. Get me to a quack.

SIMMONDS: I think you'd be better off it you went straight to bed and rested, Carter.

KENNY: Yeah. I bet you do. The last thing you want is for me to see a doctor. Well I'll tell you what. If you don't get me one right away it'll be the worse for you, because I'm going to get to a doctor one way or another. Don't you worry. I'm going to get a certified list of every bit of damage that you pricks have done to me.

SIMMONDS: Have you got any witnesses?

KENNY: How did I get like this eh? Run into a bloody door?

SIMMONDS: Went down the pub to drown your sorrows, I'd say. Got a bit sorry for yourself and started to throw your weight around.

KENNY: Fiona'll testify.

SIMMONDS: What? That I gave you a few love pats.

KENNY: She knew I was going to get bashed.

SIMMONDS: Without a doubt Carter you'd be the last of the world's great optimists. Your wife ups and leaves you without a word of warning and you think she'll get up and testify for the sake of a few of your bruises.

KENNY: She'll testify.

SIMMONDS: Look Carter, I'll strike a bargain. If I had anything of the gambler about me I wouldn't. Believe me. The odds are with us boy, make no mistake about that, because it takes an awful lot of bruises for the S.M. to take the word of a shitkicker like you against two members of the force. Nevertheless I'll strike a bargain.

KENNY: Not interested.

SIMMONDS: Believe me Carter, if I had the trace of the gambler in me makeup I'd walk out right now. Do you want to hear me out?

KENNY: No. Bugger you. I'm going to the doc in the morning.

SIMMONDS: Suit yourself. I was going to offer you something well worth considering.

KENNY: What?

SIMMONDS: If you're going to the doctor's in the morning then there's no sense discussing it.

KENNY: Don't get smart, copper.

SIMMONDS: The point is Carter, that I'm in a position to offer you something you may be needing in the next few months.

KENNY: What?

SIMMONDS: Companionship.

KENNY: *(looking at him incredulously)* Companionship?

SIMMONDS: *(realising he has been misunderstood)* Female companionship.

KENNY: *(still incredulous)* What?

SIMMONDS: Female companionship.

KENNY: You must be joking. I'm bloody near dead.

SIMMONDS: Think ahead a couple of weeks, Kenny. You've been used to getting it regularly for years.

KENNY: I can get me own women, thank you very much.

SIMMONDS: This is just to tide you over.

KENNY: *(after a pause)* What sort of women?

SIMMONDS: Well . . . er . . . there's a group of very attractive young girls a block or two from the station who . . . er . . . well, the fact is that they're very high class . . . er . . . call girls -

KENNY: *(disgusted)* Prostitutes!

SIMMONDS: *(indignant)* No. There's a world of difference between your streetwalker and your call girl, Carter. No chance of disease for a start. Safer with them than with your average wife.

KENNY: Come off it.

SIMMONDS: It's a fact.

KENNY: What? And you can get 'em for free?

SIMMONDS: I believe in well run prostitution, Carter.
It's better that they're doing it there than raping
little girls in the streets.

KENNY: What? You turn a blind eye and you get
paid off in kind?

SIMMONDS: The girls are grateful to me because I
realise their value to the community.

KENNY: You must be pretty worried to make this
sort of an offer, copper.

SIMMONDS: I don't like a big stir, Carter. That's all.

KENNY: *(bitter)* Yeah, well I'll tell you something.
I'm not going to let you pair of bludgers beat me
to a pulp and get away with it. You can sweat it
out. Now piss off. I'm going to the doctor's tomorrow.

SIMMONDS: You're a fool, Carter. Ever had a high
class call girl?

KENNY: What's so special about a harlot?

SIMMONDS: They're real performers, Carter. Real
performers.

KENNY: Piss off. You make me sick.

SIMMONDS: I can understand you wanting to get
back at me, Carter. I was playing the tough cop for
the ladies and I can understand you wanting to get
back at me; but when it's all said and done, revenge
is a mug's game, Carter. You've got nothing to show
for it in the end.

KENNY: Except satisfaction.

SIMMONDS: Satisfaction doesn't get you women,
Carter.

KENNY: *(after a pause)* How often could I get it?

SIMMONDS: Well, I'd have to see the girls, but I'd

reckon twice a week. I reckon they'd come at that.

KENNY: For how long?

SIMMONDS: As long as you need. Within reason.

KENNY: What if Fiona comes back?

SIMMONDS: I'm sorry Carter. I don't follow.

KENNY: Well, what if Fiona comes back next week? Some deal it'd be then. I'd really miss out wouldn't I? Beaten to a pulp and nothin' to show for it.

SIMMONDS: What're you getting at, Carter?

KENNY: Do they normally come to you or do you go to them.

SIMMONDS: They come to you.

KENNY: Yeah, well I want to go to them. Then it wouldn't matter if Fiona came home or not.

SIMMONDS: They don't like working at home, Carter.

KENNY: Well that's what I want.

SIMMONDS: You're pushing it a bit, Carter.

KENNY: Well what'd' you expect?

SIMMONDS: *(after a pause)* All right. I'll fix it.

KENNY: Starting Friday.

SIMMONDS: You won't be fit by Friday.

KENNY: You fix it for Friday. Takes more than a couple of mug cops to stop Kenny Carter raising the old bull moose.

SIMMONDS: Pretty quick recovery for a man who was screaming for a doctor a couple of minutes ago.

KENNY: You just fix it. Right?

SIMMONDS: All right. I'll fix it.

KENNY: And I'm no bloody fool either. I'll be along to the doc in the morning to get me a full report, and if there's the slightest hint that you're reneging on the deal then it goes straight off to Truth, complete with story.

SIMMONDS: *(grimly)* I always keep my word, Carter.

KENNY: *(looking at ROSS)* What's your mate all goggle-eyed at? *(Laughing with some effort)* Can't work out how I'm still alive eh? You'd have to be a bloody tough man to stop me, fella. *(To SIMMONDS)* What's your mate all goggle-eyed about?

SIMMONDS: *(relaxing - the hard bargainer at the conclusion of a successful deal)* It's his first day out of college. Isn't it, Ross? *(To KENNY)* Still pure at heart.

KENNY: Siddown Ross.
(ROSS, bewildered, doesn't.)
   Well, if you're not going to sit down, them make yourself useful. Grab a bloody beer from the kitchen. It'll be as hot as buggery but that's your fault for lettin' them take the fridge.

SIMMONDS: Get a beer, Ross. *(Loudly)* Get a beer!

KENNY: *(wincing)* Not so loud you bastard. Me head's still ringin'.

SIMMONDS: Sorry mate.
(ROSS goes out into the kitchen and returns with three cans of beer. He hands one to SIMMONDS and one to KENNY, who accepts it even though he looks anything but fit for drinking. SIMMONDS takes the top off his can and takes a long swig.)
   Ahh. A bit warm but not too bad. *(To KENNY)* What d'you think of Ross's potential?

KENNY: What as? A welterweight?

(He laughs with some difficulty at his own joke but he can not bring himself to drink.)

SIMMONDS: Bit worried about him actually. Should be all right. Comes from good solid stock. His father's a coffinmaker.

(They both laugh.)

KENNY: Knocks up the stiffs?

(They both laugh.)

SIMMONDS: Don't know where he gets his temper from. Should be dead calm.

KENNY: Had a bloke like him in the district reserves. Used to play ruck and forward pocket. Good player but bloody uncontrollable. Mad dog we called him. The vice-captain had to tag him some days in case he went off. Gentle as a lamb off the field but bloody lethal when he went off. Three of us would leap on the bastard. 'Cool it mad dog. It's all right'. Had to talk to him like he was a baby. Something used to click inside his head, like your mate here.

SIMMONDS: Ever gone off your head before, Ross?

ROSS: *(shyly pleased at his new notoriety)* Always had a pretty quick temper.

SIMMONDS: You'll have to watch it in future, boy. You nearly got us in the shit today.

ROSS: I'll tell you what. I've never been so scared in my life.

SIMMONDS: Well what do you think of the law in action? Eh, Ross?

KENNY: *(laughs)* He's a bit dubious about our deal.

SIMMONDS: Are you a bit dubious Ross?

ROSS: *(offhand)* No.

(He takes a swig of his beer.)

KENNY: He's waxy that you haven't lined up something for him.

SIMMONDS: Would you like that Ross?

(ROSS shrugs coyly.)

SIMMONDS: *(to KENNY)* He's a bit scared that his girlfriend will find out.

KENNY: Ah. Going steady, is he?

SIMMONDS: Oh yes. Lovely girl I believe. What's her name again, Ross?

ROSS: *(bashful)* Marilyn.

KENNY: Marilyn, eh? I knew a Marilyn once. Biggest knock in Footscray. Got your end in yet?

(ROSS shrugs.)

SIMMONDS: Won't she come across, Ross? Would you like a go at the call girls?

(ROSS shrugs, smiles and swigs.)

KENNY: Never turn down a knock, Rossy boy. Tomorrow you might get run over by a tram.

SIMMONDS: I think we've embarrassed the boy. Are you a bit confused by it all, Ross?
(ROSS shakes his head.)
Wouldn't really blame you if you were. You've crammed a lot into your first day, haven't you? Learned more today about the law and about life than you did in a whole year at College. Eh?
(ROSS shrugs.)
What you saw today's the real law, Ross. A compromise between human follies and human desires. The world is full of human beings, Ross. Remember that and you'll make a good policeman.

(ROSS looks sheepish.)

KENNY: His head's still full of those harlots.

SIMMONDS: I think the first thing you've got to do,
    Ross, is to take stock of your weakness and face
    up to them. I think it's just as well we've discovered
    this flaw in temperament of yours at an early stage
    because now that we know about it we can be sure
    that we won't place you in a situation in which you'll
    lose control. At least, not until we know you've got it
    beaten.

*(During SIMMONDS' speech ROSS'S eyes pass to
KENNY and they fix in horror as he sees that KENNY
is sitting bolt upright with a frozen look of terror and
pain in his eyes. He has just suffered a massive and
catastrophic cerebral haemorrhage as a result of his
injuries. His can drops to the floor. ROSS gets to him
just as he topples off his chair, and lowers him to the
floor. ROSS and SIMMONDS are thrown into a state
of panic akin to, but worse than, the previous one.
Worse still because they enter it from the almost
soporific sense of relief that KENNY'S death has just
shattered. For the rest of the play ROSS is hysterical
and SIMMONDS borders on this condition.)*

ROSS; Jesus, Serg. He's dead. He's really dead this
    time. You can tell. Oh Jesus!

SIMMONDS: You've done it now Ross. He's really
    dead. I didn't like the sound of it when he mentioned
    his eye. Pressure at the back of the eye is bad news,
    Ross. I thought we might've been in trouble.

ROSS: Why didn't you take him to the hospital then?
    Why didn't you take him to the hospital if you knew
    that?

SIMMONDS: They couldn't've done anything for him,
    Ross. Not a man who dies as quick as that. You

must've hit him with a bloody pile driver. He's dead,
Ross. There's no doubt about it. He's dead!

ROSS: I know he's dead! Look at the poor bastard's
eyes. He was scared out of his mind. Look at his
bloody eyes! We should've taken him straight to
hospital, Serg!

SIMMONDS: *(defensively)* They couldn't've done a
thing for him. I can tell you that right now.
Couldn't've done a thing! Not for someone who
dies as quickly as that. He was either very bad or
O.K., Ross, and if he's very bad then there's no sense
taking him to hospital. Get into casualty with a body
on your hands? I'm not crazy, Ross. I'm not callous
but then again I'm not stupid and there's an important
distinction there.

ROSS: Let's get a shotgun and make it look like suicide.
Shoot his head off. Shoot out his bloody eyes.

SIMMONDS: For Christ's sake, Ross. Don't start that
again. You're going to have to face the consequences,
I'm afraid. You're going to have to face the
consequences.

ROSS: You've got to help me, Serg! I'm no killer. I
didn't join the force to kill.
(ROSS pleads, grabbing SIMMONDS by the collar.)
For Christ's sake, Serg! You've got to help me!

SIMMONDS: *(backing away)* I'm not helping anybody,
boy. You did it!

ROSS: *(pleading, hysterical)* You're in it too Serg! You're
in it too! You let him die.

SIMMONDS: *(shouting)* He would've died in any case!

ROSS: *(advancing on SIMMONDS and pleading)* You're
in it too Serg! You've got to help me!

SIMMONDS: *(hysterical too)* I've got nothing to do with

it!

(He pushes ROSS away vigorously.)
I've got nothing to do with it!

(ROSS stands there, momentarily calmed by SIMMONDS' violence. Suddenly he runs up to SIMMONDS and hits him.)

ROSS: *(hysterical)* Sorry Serg, but you're in it too!

SIMMONDS: You mad bastard! What do you bloody think you're doing?

ROSS: *(hitting him again)* If we both get smashed up it'll look like Kenny went berserk!

SIMMONDS: *(trying to get away)* You bastard Ross! You cowardly bastard. You'll get a shit of a report from me. Mark my words!

ROSS: *(hysterical)* Hit me back, Serg! Hit me back! We'll get off! Kenny went mad and beat us both to a pulp. Hit me where it bruises. Go on Serg! You know how to bruise a man! Go on!

(ROSS advances on SIMMONDS, attacking him viciously. SIMMONDS fights back. As the play closes the fight almost takes on the air of a frenzied ritual of exorcism.)

END.